Sister
Elva,

You Have to Face It to Fix It

Best Wishe
L. Hott

You Have to Face It to Fix It

Sermons on the Challenges of Life

William D. Watley

Judson Press ® *Valley Forge*

You Have to Face It to Fix It:
Sermons on the Challenges of Life
© 1997 Judson Press, Valley Forge, PA 19482-0851

Scripture quotations in this volume are from the New Revised Standard Version of the Bible, copyright © 1989 by the Division of Christian Education of the National Council of the Churches of Christ in the United States of America. Used by permission. All rights reserved.

Library of Congress Cataloging-in-Publication Data
Watley, William D.
   You have to face it to fix it : sermons on the challenges of life / William D. Watley.
     p. cm.
   ISBN 0-8170-1267-2 (pbk. : alk. paper)
   1. Courage—Religious aspects—Christianity—Sermons. 2. Life change events—Religious aspects—Christianity—Sermons. 3. Sermons, American—Afro-American authors. 4. African Methodist Episcopal Church—Sermons. 5. Methodist Church—United States—Sermons. I. Title.
BV4647.C75W38 1997
252′.0783—dc21   97-30039

Printed in the U.S.A.

05 04 03 02 01 00 99 98 97

5 4 3 2 1

Contents

Preface

Immediately upon coming down from the mount of Transfiguration, Jesus was confronted by a father and his epileptic son. The essence of religion is not how it is experienced on the mountains of exalted worship but how it is lived in the valley of human need. The sermons in this book help us focus on the meaning and application of our faith as it relates to the personal and social issues that confront us in the valley of human need. It is my hope and prayer that these messages will be of assistance to those who are facing and fixing the various challenges of life.

There are several persons whom I must thank. First, I continue to be grateful to my sister and friend, Mrs. Carolyn Scavella, for her sensitive and competent editing skills. Second, these messages were written before I was computer literate. Therefore, much appreciation is extended to my adopted daughter, Ms. Constance Neal, for her ability to decipher my handwritten manuscripts and for her patience in preparing them for publication. Third, I am grateful to Judson Press for another publishing opportunity.

I have always dedicated my work to someone who has been a blessing to my life. This book is dedicated to one of my mentors, Dr. Roger Shinn, the distinguished Reinhold Niebuhr Professor of Social Ethics of Union Theological Seminary in New York City. Now retired, he was my major professor during my doctoral studies and without his guidance and friendship, the Ph.D. degree would have eluded me for a much longer time than it did. He continues to be a true Christian gentleman whom I shall always admire and respect.

Pax,
William D. Watley

Facing the Word of God

Text: Jonah 1:1-3

Do you have a Jonah problem? Jonah is the man in the Bible who distinguished himself by his efforts to run away from the word of God that came to him. Jonah ended up in major trouble, which will always be the case whenever we resist, disobey, or try to run from the message or revelation or command that God has given to us for our lives. Jonah received a command to go to Nineveh, the capital of the mighty Assyrian empire, and warn the people to repent of their wicked ways. The Assyrians were enemies of Jonah's people and Jonah hated them with a passion. Consequently, instead of traveling to Nineveh, Jonah hopped on a ship and headed in the opposite direction.

Jonah's problem was one of disobedience. Whenever we disobey the word of God, we have a Jonah problem. Whenever God's Word says "bring the full tithe" (Malachi 3:10) and we decide to put bills before the Waymaker, or our personal opinions or likes or dislikes before the will of almighty God, we have a Jonah problem. Whenever God gives Ten Commandments and we decide which ones we will keep and which ones we will disobey, we have a Jonah problem. When we decide that we will continue to be resentful toward people when God calls for reconciliation, or that we will continue to put prejudice above God's call for peace, or feuding above God's call for fellowship, or fighting over forgiveness, or loathing over love, or pride over prayer, we have a Jonah problem.

When we try to avoid difficult people and difficult situations instead of facing them with the Spirit of God, we have a Jonah problem. To face the Ninevites, Jonah needed to let go of hate and grow out of his prejudice, which he was not prepared to do. When we don't want to grow beyond our pettiness and small-ness—when we are content to be evil and mean-spirited, to be a fighter rather than a fixer, or to be bound rather than bountiful, or high rather than holy, or drunk rather than delivered, or a victim rather than a victor—we have a Jonah problem. When we allow what others have done to us to reduce us to their level, we have a Jonah problem. When God is saying "stop" and we are saying "go," when God is saying "go" and we are saying "no," when God is saying "my will" and we are saying "my wish," when God is saying "this way" and we are saying "my way," when God is saying "now" and we are saying "later," when God is saying "tithe" and we are saying "too much," we have a Jonah problem.

Do you have a Jonah problem? Before you answer let me remind you that God's Word says that "all have sinned and fallen short of the glory of God," and sin simply defined is disobedience to God. Sometimes we delight in talking about each other's Jonah problems and forget that every talker has a Jonah problem. Sometimes we like to debate who has the most Jonah problems and forget that there is only one Jonah prob-lem—disobedience—that is manifested in a number of ways. Sometimes we like to debate who has the worst Jonah problem or whose Jonah problem is out of control and forget that any Jonah problem can send us the wrong way.

A Jonah problem creates two problems. First, it creates dis-tance between you and God. The cold wintry weather that those of us who live in the northern hemisphere experience is a distance problem. During winter our hemisphere tilts away and moves further from the sun, thus creating distance from the source of heat. During winter the light of the sun still shines, but because we have tilted and moved away, the rays are not as powerful or warm as they are in the summer when we are closer to the sun. Thus, although the sun is still shining in the winter, the air is chilly, the weather is cold, the ground is hard, water is frozen, flowers and green grass die. The sun hasn't moved but the earth has, and the distance makes the difference between summer's heat and winter's cold.

When we have a Jonah problem, when we move away from God's Word, we create distance between us and God. The light of God's love still shines, and rays of God's blessings are all around us. But because we, and not God, have moved from obedience and tilted away from the anointing, we don't have the power to face the devil and the spirit to be victorious over our problems as we do when we are close to the source of our strength. Because we have tilted away our nights are longer. Because we have moved away our love is chilly, faith is cold, minds are hard and set in their ways, spirits are frozen, and praise has died out. Somebody once asked: "Where is the blessedness I knew when first I saw the Lord? Where is the soul's refreshing view of Jesus and his word?" They are where they've always been—we just moved and tilted. When David discovered that he had a Jonah problem and that he had moved and tilted away from God and that distance had come between them, he prayed:

Create in me a clean heart, O God,
and put a new and right spirit within me.
Do not cast me away from your presence,
and do not take your holy spirit from me.
Restore to me the joy of your salvation,
and sustain in me a willing spirit.
—Psalm 51:10-12

When we have a Jonah problem, we first create distance between ourselves and God, and then we end up in trouble. When Jonah sailed, a storm arose as he sought to do the exact opposite of what God had instructed. The sailors on the ship first sought to lighten the load of the ship by casting cargo into the sea. In the meantime Jonah had gone down into the hold of the ship and was fast asleep. The one whose disobedience had brought on the storm was asleep. The captain came to him, however, and remonstrated with him: "What are you doing sound asleep? Get up, call on your God! Perhaps the god will spare us a thought so that we do not perish." The sailors sensed that the storm was of supernatural origin. They cast lots to see who was responsible for the storm, and the lot fell upon Jonah. When he discovered that he had no choice, Jonah acknowledged who he was as the prophet of almighty God, and that he was fleeing the presence of the Lord. Jonah told the sailors to throw him overboard since he was responsible for the storm. The sailors still tried to avoid throwing Jonah overboard, but the storm grew more and more fierce. Let me just observe that some things in our lives will have to be thrown overboard before we can have peace.

When Jonah ran from God's word he found himself in a storm. Now let me hasten to add that not all storms come upon us because we have created distance between ourselves and God. Sometimes storms come precisely because we are close to the Lord. Sometimes when we are close to the Lord, the devil will send a storm to create distance between us and God. When he sends the storm then the devil will step back and say, "You're supposed to be God's child; well, look at this storm you are in. What good has all of your praying, tithing, going to church, and trying to do right gotten you? If you are God's child, why is God allowing you to go through this storm?" Well, you can tell by what happens to you in the storm whether the storm is coming because you are close or because you are distant from the Lord.

Jonah was thrown overboard because of his distance from the Lord. God has never allowed any of God's children to be thrown overboard by a storm that the devil has stirred up when that child is close to God. David declared, "I have been young and now I am old, yet I have never seen the righteous forsaken or their children begging bread" (Psalm 37:25).

Check the Scriptures and you will discover that the devil has stirred up many storms against God's children, but God has never allowed any of those children to be defeated. Even when they died, they were not defeated. John the Baptist was beheaded, but he wasn't defeated. James was slain by Herod, but he wasn't defeated. Paul was beheaded, but he wasn't defeated. Martin Luther King Jr. was shot down in Memphis, Tennessee, but he wasn't defeated.

The storm may rock your boat, but you won't be thrown overboard. The storm may wreck your boat as was the case with Paul in Acts 27. You may find yourself swimming to safety on broken pieces, but you will not be thrown overboard. So if you find yourself overboard or feel that you are about to be thrown overboard, it's time to check your distance or your closeness to God—you just may have a Jonah problem.

Jonah was thrown overboard, and the Bible says something very interesting that we often overlook in this story. The Bible tells us that "the Lord provided a large fish to swallow up Jonah" (Jonah 1:17). It doesn't say anything about a whale swallowing Jonah. A whale is not a fish but a mammal, and the

Bible doesn't say anything about a mammal, but a fish. In addition, you will not find a fish anywhere wherein a man can live for three days. That's because this fish was not a regular species but was a special creation for that man at that time. For those who doubt whether there could be such a fish, I would remind you that if you believe God is powerful enough to create a whole world big enough for everybody to live on, then God is certainly powerful enough to create one fish for one man to live in. What we are talking about is not a natural species but a miraculous creation. And I believe in a God of miracles.

"The Lord provided . . .". This fish was sent not to punish Jonah but to rescue him. It was not to be Jonah's grave in the sea but an act of God's goodness in the sea. If it had not been for the fish that God had provided, Jonah would surely have perished. When all seemed lost, God provided a fish that swallowed him up and saved him. Some of us have the same testimony. When our distance and disobedience, our sin and stubbornness and straying, our running away and our rejection of God's Word caused us to be thrown overboard and we were in danger of drowning, the Lord provided a miracle. The Lord gave us just what our own individual case and situation needed—an answer to our immediate problem, a way out of no way. When we were in danger of drowning, grace and mercy swooped us up, love and forgiveness swallowed us up, the blood of Jesus covered us up, the Holy Spirit cleaned us up, and the promises of God picked us up.

In the belly of the fish Jonah prayed. If our Jonah problem has gotten us into difficult straits, we too must pray and ask for four things. First, forgiveness. We must ask God to forgive us—for running, for the distance from God our running created, and for being overthrown because of the distance. Second, we pray for faith. Faith to believe that we are forgiven, so we are not like the Ancient Mariner, stuck where we are, going nowhere with guilt and fear hanging like an albatross around our necks. We need faith to believe God's Word—that the one who comes to God will in no way be cast out, and that if we confess our sins God is faithful and just to forgive.

Then third, we must pray for fortitude. We must pray for courage to come up from where we are and try again. We must pray for fortitude to face our futures, knowing that the same God who rescued us in times past is still in the rescuing and providing business. We must pray for fortitude to face our Ninevites, those who have wronged us, knowing that we have the victory.

When we pray for forgiveness, faith, and fortitude, we must also remember to ask for the Fortifier. Sometimes when we are faced with our Jonah problem and we must face difficult people and challenging situations, even in spite of our best intentions and efforts, forgiving power, faith, and fortitude will weaken and we will be tempted to run away. That's when we need the Fortifier.

I know such a Fortifier and his name is Jesus. He specializes in fortifying those whose forgiving power, faith, and fortitude have failed them. He knows what it is for the devil to try to overthrow you. Because of his closeness to God the devil stirred up a storm of persecution and lies, evil and violence against God and tried to overthrow God on a hill called Calvary. When Jesus died, Satan thought he had successfully overthrown him, but God provided a resting place for Jesus in Joseph of Arimethea's tomb. He stayed in that tomb all day Friday and all day Saturday, but early Sunday morning, on the third day, God raised him and so fortified Jesus that he could declare, "All power authority in heaven and on earth has been given to me" (Matthew 28:18).

Do you have a Jonah problem? I know somebody who can fix it. He's the living, resurrected, all-glorious, victorious, Word of God.

Facing God's No

Text: 2 Corinthians 12:7-10

We believers justifiably and understandably emphasize the healing miracles of the Scriptures. As we are all aware, the Bible is replete with instances of healing that come as a response to a command or prayer of faith by a believer. Our problem is that while the Bible is full of examples of God saying yes to prayer requests from believers for healing, our own lives and experience are full of examples of God saying *no* to such prayers. How do we respond when God says *no*, when as far as we can tell, based on our understanding and reading of the Scriptures, we're saying and doing all the right things? We are praying in the name of Jesus, we are praying in the name of the Father, Son, and Holy Spirit, and we have invited the Holy Spirit to come. We have touched and agreed with another believer and have bound the power of the adversary and rebuked the illness. We have fasted and prayed the prayer of faith, have been anointed with oil, and have laid on hands. We have prayed believing and expecting—and God still said *no*.

Let me say at the outset that this is a very difficult message, because I do not have the answer to the troubling questions: "Why does God say *no* sometimes? Why are some people healed and others not healed?" I have prayed for some people, and God said yes. Yet when I prayed for my own father's healing, God said *no*. God didn't say to wait; God said *no*. I find it frustrating, baffling, and painful to visit believers who truly love the Lord and to see them suffer and yet are unable to do anything about their condition. I pray for their healing, others pray for them, and God still says *no*. Then, at other times, when we are about to become completely discouraged, we pray for somebody else for whom only a miracle will do, and God says yes. We are amazed and awed again by the power of God. Why are some people healed and others who are just as deserving not healed? To put the matter personally, why are some people healed when my mother, my father, my companion, my child, my best friend are not? To put the matter even more personally, why are some people healed when *I* am not? God, why are you saying *no* to my healing?

That was the question Paul was wrestling with in the text. Paul began this chapter by talking about a momentous spiritual experience he had had in which he was taken up to heaven. He did not know whether the experience was in the body or out of the body, but while he was there, he saw and heard inexpressible things. Paul stated further that to keep him from becoming conceited about his experience in the heavenly realm, a thorn in the flesh, a messenger from Satan, was given to him to torment him. Now I do not know what the thorn was, but I believe two things: it was physical and it was painful. Thorns are painful. Paul described this spiritual experience as having taken place fourteen years earlier. We don't know when Paul started being tortured by this thorn, but if it was anytime near the experience, he had been suffering a long time.

As a good believer, Paul took his thorn to God in prayer not once or twice but three times. Paul repeatedly prayed, pleaded, promised, and agonized with God to heal him, to take the thorn from him. And guess what? God said *no*. Could God possibly say *no* to Paul whom he had taken to heaven and to whom he had revealed the inexpressible? Could God possibly say *no* to Paul whose life he had turned around on the Damascus road and whose feet he had put on a street called Straight? Paul was blinded during his conversion experience. He was healed of his blindness, but God said *no* to the removal of the thorn. At the beginning of Acts 28 we read that Paul was shipwrecked on the island of Malta and was bitten by a poisonous snake—a viper fastened itself onto Paul's hand. Paul shook it off in the fire and went about his business. He didn't swell up and he didn't die. The Bible doesn't even say that he prayed for healing, yet he was healed. He was healed of a snakebite that the Bible doesn't even tell us he prayed over, yet God said *no* when he prayed over his thorn.

During his own ministry Paul was empowered to heal others. In Lystra he healed a man crippled from birth. In Ephesus he cast out a demon from a tormented girl, and in Troas he restored life to a young man believed to be dead. Yet his own thorn was not healed. When he and Silas were locked in jail, they prayed and sang so powerfully that the earth shook, the prison doors flew open, and their chains fell off. Yet when he prayed about his own thorn, nothing happened.

After God said *no* to Paul, God said *instead*. When God says *no*, look for God's *instead*. God never says *no* without an *instead*—a substitute, another blessing, another answer, another revelation, another solution, another way. God said *no* to Moses: "You will not enter the Promised Land. *Instead*, I will transport you across the barriers of time and put you on the snow-kissed crest of Mount Hermon to speak with my Son, Jesus, the fulfillment of the Law, who is about to give his life as a ransom for many." When David's son by Bathsheba was stricken with illness and David prayed and fasted for the child's life, God said *no* to David's prayer, and the child died. Later, when Bathsheba became pregnant again, God said yes, and Solomon was born. The writer of Hebrews tells us in Hebrews 11 that many of the faithful died without having received the promise. Instead God prepared for them a better country, a heavenly one.

When God says *no*, look for the *instead*. That's just a fancy way of saying what the old preachers used to say: "God will never close a door without opening up a window." Let me rephrase that: God will never close a window without opening up a door. Often that which God opens for us and does for us, with us, and through us after a *no* is broader, deeper, taller, and more wonderful than the narrowness of our request.

God said *no* to Paul's request; instead the Lord spoke to him and said, "My grace is sufficient for you" (2 Corinthians 12:9). Why grace? The Lord could easily have said, "My love (or peace or will or salvation) is sufficient." Why grace? Let's remember what grace is. Grace is the unsought, unasked for, and unmerited goodness of God. Grace is what God does for us without our asking. We ask for blessings, forgiveness, and peace, but grace is what God gives because God is good—all the time. When God says *no*, God is saying, "I will give you what you need without your asking for it." When you have a thorn, you may not know what to ask for. The pain may be so acute, the heartbreak and sorrow may be so piercing, the burden may be so heavy, that you may ask for relief or release in any way, even death. But remember, even without your knowing what to ask for, God will still take care of you.

I once went to see a church member who had been hospitalized several times. This individual was not simply a church member but was a true believer in the Word of God. We had been praying for him very earnestly. He went to the very threshold of death and recovered enough to return to church once again to worship, but after that he suffered a relapse and was again staring death in the face. When I went to visit him in the hospital, he didn't even recognize me. I remembered that he had asked the Lord not to take his presence of mind away so that he would not find himself unable to call on the name of the Lord. So I asked God, "Why would you let him get this way? His greatest desire was that he have presence of mind to worship you." But as I was preparing this sermon, I felt as if the Lord was speaking to me and saying, "Without their asking, I will take care of my own. Whether this believer has presence of mind to call upon me or not, I'm still taking care of him. He's still in my hands." When God says *no*, remember God's grace is still sufficient. God takes care of you even without your asking.

I could end the sermon here with these words: "My grace is sufficient." Just knowing that without my asking, God is going to bless me, keep me, protect me, feed me, and watch over me when I'm helpless is enough for me to shout my way, pray my way, and fight my way to victory. But that is not all the Lord said. The Lord also told Paul: "[My] power is made perfect in weakness" (2 Corinthians 12:9). In other words, the Lord says,

> After I say *no*, not only will I continue to take care of you, but my power will still work through you even in your diminished capacity and weakened condition. Because you are weak, my power can compensate for anything you lack on your own. What I will do in you will be all the more glorious and all the more miraculous because you are weak. I know you desire to have all eight cylinders. I'm going to leave you with only four, but when I get through with the four you have left, that four will do as much as eight. My power is made perfect in weakness.

This Paul, the one who had the thorn that God didn't remove, wrote or influenced fourteen of the twenty-seven books of the New Testament, logged more miles in his travels, and established more churches than anyone else in the Bible. He is quoted more often than anyone except Jesus. "My power is made perfect in weakness."

One of the most dynamic preachers I have ever known was a frail, wheelchair-bound, one-hundred-pound man with crippling arthritis and heart disease. But when he began to sing, with his broken body and gnarled hands, "His Eye Is on the Sparrow," he had the strength of a Samson. "My power is made perfect in weakness."

The great invitational hymn that has probably brought more souls to Christ than any hymn ever written, "Just As I Am," was composed by Charlotte Elliot, an invalid who was bedridden for fifty years. "My power is made perfect in weakness."

See blind Fanny Crosby writing "Blessed Assurance," "Pass Me Not," "Jesus Keep Me Near the Cross," "I Am Thine O Lord," "To God Be the Glory," "Close to Thee," "Savior More Than Life to Me," and over five thousand other hymns. "My power is made perfect in weakness."

See sightless Milton writing about paradise or deaf Beethoven composing symphonies or near-deaf Thomas Edison perfecting the phonograph. "My power is made perfect in weakness."

When Paul realized all that God's power could do through him, no wonder he moved off "Complaining Avenue" onto "Praise Boulevard" and said, "Therefore I am content with weaknesses, insults, hardships, persecutions, and calamities for the sake of Christ; for whenever I am weak, then I am strong" (2 Corinthians 12:10).

Facing Your Difficulties with God

Text: Jeremiah 12:1

One of the great truths that we have heard preached, proclaimed, testified to, and sung about over and over again is that God will neither fail us nor forsake us. Another great truth that we have been taught is that God will hear and answer prayer. Yet the truth is that a number of us have felt forsaken by God. There have been times when we have felt that God has failed us. There have been times when we have felt that God has not answered our prayers. There have been times when we have been disappointed, frustrated, and even angry with God. Sometimes believing in God "ain't so easy."

Although it's often kept quiet, a number of us who outwardly appear to be the strongest, most pious, well-grounded, and self-assured have difficulties with God. We don't talk about our difficulties because we don't want to appear to be infidels, disbelievers, or ungrateful. Or we don't want to offend or make God angry. All of our lives we have been taught not to doubt or question God. And yet in our heart of hearts we do have questions and disappointments and difficulties, and sometimes even anger with God. And because of these questions, difficulties, disappointments, and residual anger, we don't feel as close to God as we'd like and we are not as sure or secure in our relationship with God as we would like to be or as others seem to be.

If our relationship with God is to be what we really want it to be; if we are to feel as close to God as we would like, if we would have the kind of relationship with God that others claim they have, or that we see portrayed in the Bible, one of the issues that we need to face so that it can be fixed is our difficulties, disappointments, anger, frustrations, and questions that we would like to put before God. We will never grow close to God unless we are honest about our problems with God.

I'm going to say something that will shock many of you because it goes against one of the cornerstone beliefs that we have been brought up with and have heard all of our lives. That statement is this: It's all right to question God. Not only is it all right, it's healthy to question God. It's all right because, first, God knows everything, especially us, and God knows about our questions. Not asking doesn't mean that they are not there. It only means that we are burying them, submerging them, hiding them, pretending they are not there, covering them up under a religious facade or form.

Second, it's all right to question God because there is a difference between questioning God and doubting God. We often confuse questioning God and doubting God. When we doubt, we are saying, "I'm not sure if I believe." When we question we're saying, "I believe—I just don't understand." Doubt says, "I'm not sure if you are real or true." Questions say, "I know that you are real and true; I just don't understand why you do what you do." Doubts are like termites that eat away at the foundation of a house. Questions are like repairmen fixing up a house. Doubts are like the breakdown of an engine. Questions are like a tune-up of an engine. Doubts are critical care; questions are corrective surgery. Doubts lead to confusion, but questions lead to understanding.

It's all right to question God, third, because we learn only by asking questions. When two people are trying to build a relationship, they have to ask questions about each other's likes and dislikes, each other's habits, and each other's opinions. Those of us who remember the *Star Wars* movie series are familiar with the phrase "May the Force be with you." God is more than some force or energy field that's with me. God is a personality with whom I can build a relationship and to whom I can get close. God is more than a something—God is Somebody. And when you build a relationship with Somebody, when you really want to get to know Somebody, sometimes you're going to have to ask questions. Remember, questions are not about doubting but about learning and understanding.

It's all right to question God because, fourth, God can handle our questions. If God can handle our sins and disobedience, God can handle our questions. If God can handle our broken promises and forgotten vows, then God can handle our questions. If God can handle our weaknesses, faults, failings, and backsliding, then God can handle our questions. Our lives are greater insults to God than our questions. Our gossip and our pettiness are greater insults to God than our questions. Our selfishness and stubbornness are greater insults to God than our questions. Our phoniness and hypocrisy are greater insults to God than our questions. If God can handle everything we are not and still love us, if our daily sins do not cause God to lose patience with us and strike us off the face of the earth, then God is able to love us in spite of our questions.

God is not some fragile glass dish that we must protect. God is not some temperamental, short-tempered old tyrant who is easily insulted and offended and will strike us down or punish us or withhold blessings at the slightest provocation. God is patient and long suffering, forgiving and understanding. So God can handle our questions, our difficulties, our frustrations, and problems as they arise in our relationship with God.

It's all right to question God because, fifth, some of the most powerful personalities in Scripture had questions at one time or another. That's how they became so close to God. That's how they could remain faithful. When they had difficulties with God, they faced them so that they could be fixed. They didn't pretend that they didn't have them. They were not afraid to express them. They understood that if their relationship with God was going to grow, they would have to open up rather than cover up their difficulties. That's what Jeremiah was doing in this text. Jeremiah had some difficulties with God, so he brought them to God in order that they might be fixed. In so many words, he said,

> God, I know that you are always right, and I know that you
> know how to run your business. But as one of your servants,
> there are some questions I have about the way you run your
> business. I know that you are not obligated to explain your
> business to me, but as your servant trying to do your will, I
> could work a little better and feel a little closer to you if you

would clarify something that's been bothering me. Why does the way of the guilty thrive? Why do all who are treacherous thrive? Or in other words, why do evil people get along so well?

Jeremiah continued,

They couldn't do it, God, without you. You plant them, and they take root; they grow and bring forth fruit; you are near in their mouths, yet far from their hearts. But you, O Lord, know me; you see me and test me: my heart is with you. I'm serving you, I love you, so why are you so hard on me, while they are living "high on the hog"?

The books of Jeremiah and Lamentations are full of the questions of this prophet. He is in a long line of faithful and believing servants who openly questioned God. Abraham was the father of the faithful. Yet when God told Abraham that he and Sarah would have a son in their old age, according to Genesis 17:17, Abraham fell on his face and laughed in God's face and asked, "Can a child be born to a man who is a hundred years old? Can Sarah, who is ninety years old, bear a child?" When Moses was called to free the Israelites from Egyptian bondage, he not only questioned God as to what, how, and when, but he then asked God to send somebody else. Job may have endured his suffering but not without asking God "why" over and over again. The psalms are full of the questions of David, the man after God's own heart. In Psalm 10 he asks, "Why, O Lord, do you stand far off? Why do you hide yourself in times of trouble?" If Jonah hadn't had questions he wouldn't have run away. Hear the prophet Habakkuk: "O Lord, how long shall I cry for help, and you will not listen? Or cry to you 'Violence!' and you will not save?" (Habakkuk 1:2).

John the Baptist, powerful preacher that he was, had his questions and difficulties with Jesus and asked him, "Are you he who is to come or shall we look for another?" (Matthew 11:3). According to Revelation 6:10, the souls of slaughtered saints under the altar in heaven asked God, "Sovereign Lord, holy and true, how long will it be before you judge and avenge our blood on the inhabitants of the earth?" Even Jesus on Calvary quoted his ancestor David, who in Psalm 22 asked, "My God, my God, why have you forsaken me?" (v. 1). None of these people were faithless. Their questions were a reflection of their effort to grow.

So if you find yourself asking questions of God, know that you are in good company.

When Jeremiah asked his questions, God did not answer him directly. When we read the Scriptures we note that most of those who questioned God did not receive direct answers. Yet they continued to believe. It's all right to question God because, sixth, faith is not faith unless it has some questions. In other words, faith is not simply swallowing everything hook, line, and sinker. Faith is not about having everything worked out in a neat little package, or wrapped up in some surefire formula that will work all the time, that has everything settled, all questions answered, all issues resolved. Faith is not getting everything you pray for every time. It doesn't take faith to believe in God if God does everything we want God to do when we want God to do it, the way we want God to do it. "For who hopes for what is seen? But if we hope for what we do not see, we wait for it with patience" (Romans 8:24-25).

Faith doesn't mean we have no questions. Faith means believing with questions and all. Faith means that when God says yes, we believe. And when God says no, we believe. And when we don't know what God is saying, still we believe. Faith means believing when we understand and believing when we don't understand. Faith means believing in the bright daylight, and believing in the darkest midnight. Faith means believing when there is not a cloud in the sky, and in the midst of the storm. Faith means believing when the water is clear and sparkling, and when the water is muddy and murky.

Faith is Job's declaring, "Though he slay me yet will I trust him" (Job 13:15). Faith is Habakkuk's saying, "Though the fig tree does not blossom, and no fruit is on the vines; though the produce of the olive fails and the fields yield no food; though the flock is cut off from the fold and there is no herd in the stalls, yet I will rejoice in the LORD, I will exult in the God of my salvation" (Habakkuk 3:17-18). Faith is Jesus' saying in Gethsemane, "Nevertheless not my will but your will be done. However you work it out, I'll be satisfied." Faith is Jesus' continuing to hang on Calvary's cross even though his question is not answered.

Some may wonder how we keep a faith that believes even when our questions are not answered. First, we trust the purposes of God. I don't know why God does some things or allows some things to happen, but I believe God has a reason. I trust God's purposes. Paul put it like this: we know that "all things work together for good for those who love God, who are called according to his purpose" (Romans 8:28). The eighteenth-century poet William Cowper put it like this in his poem "Light Shining Out of Darkness": "God moves in a mysterious way his wonders to perform, plants his footsteps on the sea and rides upon the storm." God is too wise to make mistakes and too right to do wrong. So even though we have our questions we trust the providence and purposes of God.

We can believe in God even with our questions when we trust the promises of God. God promised that though the mountains may depart and the hills be removed, his steadfast love shall not depart from us. God promised to supply all of our needs according to God's riches in glory. God promised that the righteous would live by faith, the wicked would cease from troubling, and the weary would be at rest. God promised not to be slack concerning God's promises.

We can believe in God even with our questions when we trust the purposes of God, the promises of God, and finally the provisions of God. That simply means that we know God is going to take care of us. We don't know why our loved one died, but we know God is going to take care of us. We don't know why we lost our job, but we know God is going to take care of us. We don't know why our relationship or marriage fell apart, but we know God is going to take care of us. We don't know what's going to happen to our children, but we put them in God's hands, and so we know God is going to take care of us. We don't know why God won't heal us, but we know God is going to take care of us. We don't know where the money will come from to pay our bills, but we know God is going to take care of us. We don't know what the future holds, but we know God is going to take care of us.

Facing Your Enemies

Text: Acts 9:10-19

What is an enemy? Someone who has hurt us? An enemy is not simply someone who does or says something against us. A lot of people, including friends and family, can do and say things against us, but a person only becomes an enemy when what that person says or does causes us pain that we can't just shake off. You have to feel something for an enemy. It may be dislike, loathing, hatred, disdain, or disgust, but you have to exert some passion and energy on an enemy. We've all heard the saying, "Sticks and stones may break my bones, but words will never hurt me." Not so with an enemy. The words of an enemy hurt. An enemy, then, is somebody who has gotten inside of our head and our heart.

All of us have enemies. All of us have people who have hurt us and all of us have hurt someone. The latter truth is what we are inclined to forget. We can remember all the dirt that has been thrown upon us, but we've done our share of mudslinging, cutting, and being petty. A preacher once broke up fight and when he asked how it started, one of the boys said: "He hit me and I hit him back, then he hit me and I hit him." At some point it makes no difference who started the fight if the fight is the only reason that both people are keeping it going. At a certain point one person is as guilty as the other. You are not obligated to keep a fight going simply because somebody started it five, ten, or twenty years ago. Often when we start trying to determine who started the fight, so much misunderstanding and miscommunication has taken place that we can't figure out the point at which enmity started building up between people. One person tracks the problem to one incident or place or person or time, while the other person focuses on a different incident. Often the war was taking place in the head and heart long before it broke out in the open.

We all have enemies because we make some ourselves. Sometimes we may not intend to hurt people but we do; other times we know just what we are doing. Then again sometimes we have enemies because others set themselves up as our enemies.

In some cases people will dislike us if we represent in their eyes what they are not. I used to say that people will not hate you without cause. I've learned over the years not to make that statement. There's always a cause. It may not be a good one, it may not be one we can do anything about, it may be one that neither we nor they can put our finger on, but there's always a cause:

"I don't like that person."

"Why?"

"I don't know, I just don't."

Jealousy and insecurity are two of the basic reasons people become enemies. If a person is insecure and doesn't like himself or herself, and you are self-confident, that person will dislike you. If a person doesn't like his or her looks and considers you attractive, that person may dislike you. If a person is weak in body and you are healthy, that person may dislike you. If a person is not very popular and you are popular, that person may dislike you. If a person is not very smart or just average and you are very smart, that person may dislike you. If a person is lazy and you're doing things, that person may dislike you. If a person doesn't have much and you have a lot, that person may dislike you. If a person is in his or her declining years and you are young and have the best years ahead of you, that person may dislike you. Sometimes people are your enemies because they don't like themselves, and it's easier for them to hurt you than it is for them to experience inner healing.

We have enemies because we make some ourselves. We have enemies because some people set themselves up as our enemies. Then we have enemies because the devil is going to give us some, particularly if we are trying to serve the Lord and live a decent life. The devil is going to put people in our lives to try our spirit and our patience, sap our joy, break our determination, and turn us around. Sometimes we wonder what we have done to make people dislike us. Well, if we have vision, we're trying to do the right thing, we're nice to others, we're trying to lead others to Christ. That's enough for the devil to dislike us and raise up foes to defeat us. And the devil is smart enough to use those closest to us, because he realizes that termites can do more damage to a house eating away on the inside than woodpeckers can do on the outside. The only way to avoid making the devil your enemy is to want nothing worthwhile, do nothing worthwhile, become nothing worthwhile, stand for nothing worthwhile, talk about nothing worthwhile, think about nothing worthwhile, live for nothing worthwhile, and die for nothing worthwhile.

We all have enemies—even Jesus did. He got his the same way we get ours. Some he made. Statements to the effect that prostitutes and tax collectors would enter the kingdom before Pharisees and Sadducees, and his calling these religious leaders hypocrites, blind guides, and whitewashed tombs in Matthew 23 are not things that make friends of our enemies. Then the Pharisees and Sadducees did their part to keep the gap wide by trying to undermine everything Jesus did, because they were jealous of the masses that heard him gladly. Further, because the devil knew what would happen to him if Jesus ever succeeded, he set up a host of enemies, including outsiders like the Roman government and the religious hierarchy and insiders like Jesus' trusted disciples and family members like his own brothers and sisters.

In today's text Ananias, who was a devoted follower of Jesus, was being asked to do one of the hardest things that he would ever be asked to do. Ananias was instructed to face an enemy and heal him. An overbearing and overzealous Saul had disrupted the church in Jerusalem and was on his way to Damascus to do the same thing. On the Damascus Road that led to the city, however, Saul experienced the risen Christ who asked him, "'Saul, Saul, why do you persecute me?' He asked, 'Who are you, Lord?' The reply came, 'I am Jesus, whom you are persecuting. But get up and enter the city, and you will be told what you are to do'" (Acts 9:4-6). After the heavenly visitation, Saul was blinded. For three days and three nights he was without sight and ate and drank nothing.

When bad things happen to our enemy, we typically react by saying, "Uh huh! No better for them. God don't like ugly."

While we may not wish for the misfortune of people who have hurt us, when something bad happens to them, we can't help but feel that they are getting what they deserve. Can't you just hear Ananias: "Heal him? Do you know who Saul is? Have you forgotten what he did to the church in Jerusalem? Isn't he here in Damascus to do the same thing? Heal him?! We've been praising you because he is blind. We thought that the blindness was a blessing from you to protect us." But hear God's word to Ananias: "Go, for he is an instrument whom I have chosen to bring my name before Gentiles and kings and before the people of Israel; I myself will show him how much he must suffer for the sake of my name" (vv. 15-16).

In other words, before Ananias could face Saul, God had to prepare Ananias's heart and frame of mind. Before we can face our enemies with the right spirit we have to ask God to first prepare us. Perhaps that's why we have so little success in dealing with our enemies. We are so busy praying over them and about them and asking the Lord to fix them that we fail to ask God to fix us. You cannot face an enemy who has hurt you deeply under your own power. There is too much hurt that hasn't been healed, too much misunderstanding and confusion that hasn't been cleared up, too much resentment that wants to be satisfied and avenged. When we have been hurt, it's natural to want to inflict pain on the person responsible.

That's why we have to ask Jesus to prepare us to face our enemies. We have to come clean and confess:

> Lord, I know what your Word says, but I cannot face this person on my own strength. I cannot forgive this person by my own power. I need you to do something within me. I need a new heart. I need a new attitude. I need some new thoughts. I need you to direct my words. I need you to correct my motives. I need you to help me select the right time. Even if the field has been prepared for the seed, I need you to make me physically fit and ready to work in the field. Lord, I need you to work on me.

It's hard to pray that prayer when we are relating to an enemy, because our tendency is to see everything that's wrong with the enemy. But if what's wrong between us and someone else is to be fixed, then we have to face ourselves and ask the Lord to fix us.

Ananias was hesitant because of what Saul had done. Saul's blindness, however, was an indication that God had him under control. Sometimes we are fearful about facing enemies. We don't want to go certain places because we might run into certain people. We walk around looking over our shoulders, afraid that our enemies are behind us. The lesson reminds us that not only was Ananias in God's hands, but Saul, his enemy, was under God's control. That's why we need not fear our enemies. The same hand that holds us controls them. The same hand that makes ways for us so that we can walk through the Red Sea on dry ground clogs Pharaoh's chariot wheels in the mud when he comes in behind us. The same eyes that are watching over us are also watching them. That's why our walk needs to be close to the Lord, because when we walk close to the Lord, our enemies can't get but so close to us.

Following heaven's instructions, Ananias went to the house where Saul was staying, laid his hands upon him and said, "Brother Saul, the Lord Jesus, who appeared to you on your way here, has sent me so that you may regain your sight and be filled with the Holy Spirit" (v. 17). Immediately Saul's eyesight was restored.

If you ask the Lord to prepare you first, and if you understand that you have nothing to fear because no enemy is bigger than our God, then the Lord will make you bigger than your enemies, because the Lord has prepared you. And because the Lord has prepared you, instead of trying to break your enemies, you will end up blessing them. Just knowing that you have the victory will be reward enough. The Lord will help you to heal rather than hurt, bless rather than battle, and pray for them rather than persecute them.

Consider the story of Joseph in Genesis. We will be able to say to those who have hurt us deeply, as Joseph did to his brothers who sold him into slavery, "You meant it for evil, but God meant it for good" (Genesis 50:20, paraphrased). You need help facing enemies. The same Jesus who helped Ananias, who prepared Ananias, who gave Ananias the victory, who put healing in the hands of Ananias, is able to help you.

Facing the Devil

Text: Luke 22:39-44

All three of the Synoptic Gospels (Matthew, Mark, and Luke) record the agony of Jesus in the garden of Gethsemane. Only Luke tells us, however, that during his prayer Jesus was strengthened by an angel and that Jesus prayed so earnestly that his sweat became like great drops of blood falling to the ground. The only other instance in the Gospels in which an angel comes and ministers to Jesus—that I can recall—is after Jesus' temptation by Satan in the wilderness at the beginning of his ministry. I believe that an angel came to Jesus in Gethsemane to strengthen him because our Lord was again under attack by the Adversary. At some point in our lives, every child of God is going to have to face the devil, the biblical symbol for evil. What are the lessons that we learn from observing Jesus' confrontation with the devil in Gethsemane?

We first observe that Jesus fought the devil in private. Although he took Peter, James, and John with him into the garden, he left them at a certain point and went off by himself. Second, as he was praying, they were sleeping. Thus this fight, like the one in the desert at the beginning of Jesus' ministry, was not a public but a private encounter. We don't fight the devil in public but in private. We may have to fight the devil's temptations in public, but the outcome of that public confrontation depends upon how we did with our private battle with Satan. The fight with evil is about the control of our mind and our spirit—and that's a private battle. Before the devil can get you to fall publicly, he must first capture your mind and spirit in private. When do you face Satan? Whenever a wrong thought or desire enters the privacy of your mind and spirit. When that wrong thought or desire comes into the privacy of your mind and spirit, you have to decide whether you will fight the devil or run with the devil. Nobody can observe the devil capturing your mind and binding your spirit. That is done internally in the privacy of your thoughts and in the secret yielding of your spirit.

Judas was in the very presence of the disciples at the Last Supper when according to the Scriptures, Satan entered him—but nobody saw Satan enter. Nobody even knew about it but Jesus. Jesus alone knew, even as Judas sat at the table, that Judas had already yielded to Satan. You can have an image of holiness in public and still be fighting a private war with Satan that nobody knows about but you, Satan, and Jesus. That is our hope for our private fights, that Jesus knows what's going on inside and Jesus is ready to help us if we call on his name. That's why he told Peter, "Simon, Simon, listen! Satan has demanded to sift all of you like wheat, but I have prayed for you that your own faith may not fail; and you, when once you have turned back, strengthen your brothers" (Luke 22:31). Remember in your private battles that Jesus knows all about your inner struggles. And if you ask him, he's prepared to "guide till the day is done."

You can't fight a cold in public. The only thing you can do is spread a cold in public. The only way you can fight a cold is go to bed and rest, so the immune and defense systems in your body can do the fighting. When you try to fight the devil in public, the only thing you do is spread the devil. You have to come apart and yield to God so that God's immune systems that are in you—the power of God's name, the covering of God's blood, the promises of God's Word, the anointing of God's Spirit, God's goodness and mercy—can come to your defense.

Jesus not only fought the devil privately, but he fought him in prayer. You can't out*run* the devil, you can't out*talk* the devil, out*think* the devil, out*trick* the devil, out*politic* the devil, out*buy* the devil, out*sing* the devil, out*read* the devil, out*shout* the devil, out*work* the devil. Your only defense against the devil is to out*pray* him.

Someone has said that the strongest demon in hell trembles when the weakest Christian prays. The reason is simple. What happened to Jesus in our text also happens to us when we pray. When Jesus prayed, an angel, a representative of the heavenly host, came to strengthen him. When we pray, we need to know that the heavenly host responds. Daniel prayed and an angel gave hungry lions lockjaw (Daniel 6:22). Three Hebrew boys prayed and one who had the appearance of a son of God joined them in the fiery furnace (Daniel 3:25). Hezekiah prayed and an angel slew 85,000 Assyrian troops (2 Kings 19:15ff, 35). Elijah prayed and both fire and rain fell from heaven (1 Kings 18:36-38). Jehoshaphat prayed and confusion broke out in the enemy camp (2 Chronicles 20:18-23). Paul and Silas prayed and an earthquake shook their dungeons (Acts 16:25-26). The early church prayed and an angel set Peter free (Acts 12:5-11).

When we pray, the heavenly host comes to our rescue. Jeremiah calls out: "The steadfast love of the Lord never ceases, his mercies never come to an end; they are new every morning; great is your faithfulness" (Lamentations 3:22-23). Isaiah comes forth and says, "Thou will keep him in perfect peace whose mind is stayed on Thee because he trusts in Thee" (Isaiah 26:3). David testifies: "Even though I walk through the valley of the shadow of death, I fear no evil; for you are with me; your rod and your staff, they comfort me" (Psalm 23:4). Paul stands up and says, "I can do all things through Christ who strengthens me" (Philippians 4:3). The writer of Hebrews reminds us: "Let us hold on to the profession of our faith without wavering" (Hebrews 10:23). From way out on Patmos, John declares: "I was in the Spirit on the Lord's day" (Revelation 1:10). When we pray Jesus intercedes, the Holy Spirit anoints, and God sends angels to minister to us.

Jesus fought the devil privately. He fought him in prayer. Then he fought him with persistence. There is no such thing as a onetime, knockout punch with the devil. That's where some of us make our mistakes. We believe that once beaten, always beaten. The devil only leaves us for a season. You can beat him today and if you are not prayerful, he will come back with the same test and temptation and can beat you tomorrow. The devil is persistent; the only way you can beat him is to be more persistent than he. That is why Jesus was praying so earnestly that sweat poured off him. He was as persistent for us as the devil was against us. He was as persistent for our salvation as the devil was for our damnation. He was as persistent for our victory as the devil was for our defeat. He was as persistent for our elevation as the devil was for our degradation.

The good news that I bring is that Jesus' persistence won out. He persisted so much that the mob that arrested him could not intimidate him; Judas's betrayal of him, Peter's denial of him, and the disciples' desertion of him didn't embitter him; Herod couldn't humiliate him; Pilate couldn't condemn him; a cross couldn't break him; the grave couldn't hold him. He was so persistent that he now reigns as King of kings and Lord of lords.

Somebody once said that with persistence the slowest turtle and the smallest snail eventually reached Noah's Ark. I know that sometimes it doesn't seem as if we are making progress, but if we persist in the name of Jesus, we shall get the victory over Satan. Ain't no mountain high enough, ain't no valley low enough, ain't no river wide enough, ain't no devil strong enough to keep God's power and Spirit from breaking through to a child of God who persists in prayer.

When I was a little boy I used to hear the old folk sing:

Lord, I have started to walk in the light
Shining upon me from heaven so bright;
I bade the world and its follies adieu,
I started in, Jesus, and I'm going through.

I'm going thro', yes, I'm going thro',
I'll pay the price, whatever others do;
I'll take the way with the Lord's despised few.
I'm going thro', Jesus, I'm going thro'.[1]

---

1. From "I'm Going Through, Jesus," p.d.

Facing Your Fears

Text: 1 Kings 19:13-14

Several years ago there was a well-known television circus show that featured a Bengal tiger act. Like the rest of the show, the act was done live before a large audience. One evening, the tiger trainer went into the cage with several tigers to do a routine performance. The door was locked behind him. The spotlights highlighted the cage, the television cameras moved in close, and the audience watched in suspense as the trainer skillfully put the tigers through their paces. In the middle of the performance, the worst possible fate befell the act: the lights went out! For twenty or thirty long, dark seconds the trainer was locked in with the tigers. In the darkness they could see him, but he could not see them. A whip and a small kitchen chair seemed meager protection under the circumstances, but he survived, and when the lights came on, he calmly finished the performance. In an interview afterward, he was asked how he felt knowing that the tigers could see him but that he could not see them. He first admitted the chilling fear of the situation, but pointed out that the tigers did not know that he could not see them. He said, "I just kept cracking my whip and talking to them until the lights came on. And they never knew I could not see them as well as they could see me."

This experience gives us a vivid parable of human life. At some point in our lives, all of us face the terrifying task of fighting tigers in the dark. Some face it constantly. Many people cope daily with internal problems that are capable of destroying them. They cannot visualize their problems or understand them, but their problems seem to have them zeroed in.[1]

What are the tigers in the dark in your life? Things that go bump in the night and cause us to lose sleep, things that we perceive have the potential to destroy us. That's what fear is—something that we perceive has the potential to destroy us. Whether the tigers are real, as in the case of the story, or figments of our imagination is beside the point. If we perceive them to be real, then for us perception is reality.

Fear is fear and if a person is afraid of something or someone, that fear can be just as immobilizing and paralyzing and can have as much potential for self-destruction whether the tiger they fear is real or imaginary. Telling somebody not to be afraid won't solve the problem. People are afraid not because they desire to be afraid, but because they do not know how not to be afraid. If they knew how not to be afraid they wouldn't be afraid. People who have phobias or fear of certain things such as heights, closed-in places, all animals or certain animals, people in general or certain people, the future, failure, water, flying, driving, storms, death, and so forth, do not want to be afraid of certain things. They do not know how not to be afraid.

Telling someone that he or she has nothing to fear does not solve the problem because fear has its own logic. "A royal Bengal tiger, kept at the Residency Calcutta, exhibited the greatest fear at the sight of a mouse. If the mouse moved about, the tiger ran or sprang away, as if in dread of destruction. The tiger could have crushed the mouse with a blow from its mighty paw or foot. But the tiger's fear blocked out all logic and blinded him to the truth." Fear can distort reality, deaden you to common sense, deaden your reasoning faculties and blind you to the truth. You cannot see things as they are except through your fear.[2]

Telling someone that he or she has nothing to fear but fear itself is good rhetoric but bad medicine, because fear itself is a deadly enemy that can destroy you.

According to an ancient legend, a man driving one day to Constantinople was stopped by an old woman who asked him for a ride. He took her up beside him and, as they drove along, he looked at her and became frightened and asked, "Who are you?"

The old woman replied: "I am Cholera." Thereupon the peasant ordered the old woman to get down and walk; but she persuaded him to take her along upon her promise that she would not kill more than five people in Constantinople. As a pledge of the promise she handed him a dagger, saying to him that it was the only weapon with which she could be killed. Then she added: "I shall meet you in two days. If I break my promise, you may stab me."

In Constantinople 120 people died of cholera. The enraged man who had driven her to the city, and to whom she had given the dagger as a pledge that she would not kill more than five persons, went out to look for the old woman, and meeting her, raised his dagger to kill her. But she stopped him, saying: "I have kept my agreement. I killed only five. Fear killed the others."[3]

Either we learn to control and live with our tigers in the dark or our fears will control us and destroy us. Either we face our fears and fix them or our fears will fix us. This text is an illustration of this truth. Elijah had won a great victory for God on Mount Carmel. He had outprayed 450 prophets and 400 prophets of Asherah, who were Canaanite gods that had a number of followers but no power. Elijah had prayed fire down from heaven on Mount Carmel, and then had prayed rain down from the same skies to end a three-and-a-half-year drought. Even though the prophets of Asherah and Baal had Elijah hopelessly outnumbered, and even though they prayed from morning until evening, they had produced nothing but their own perspiration and fatigue.

After the supremacy of Yahweh, the true and living God, had been reestablished, the people who had gathered on Mount Carmel revolted against the prophets of Baal and Asherah. When King Ahab, who was present on Mount Carmel, told his queen, Jezebel, of Elijah's actions, she swore to take Elijah's life within twenty-four hours. When Elijah heard of Queen Jezebel's threat, great man of God that he was, and persevering prayer warrior, he "lost it" and ran away to the wilderness.

Let us note two things about Elijah's flight. First, many have made much of the fact that Elijah had stood up to over 850 men on Mount Carmel but ran away from one woman named Jezebel. Logic would say that the 850 men had more potential to destroy Elijah than Jezebel. Whether they did or not is beside the point. In Elijah's mind Jezebel was a greater threat than the 850 he had withstood. You can be bold about many things and brave before many foes, and yet cower and panic before one thing. In other words, you don't need a lot of tigers in the dark, just one in your cage to get you on the run. People who say that they are not afraid of anything are doing one of two things—either bluffing or they just haven't met the right tiger.

Second, Elijah, who was the epitome of boldness and fearlessness, panicked and ran. Everybody can lose it at some point. No matter how many tigers you have faced and withstood in the past, the right tiger at the right moment can cause you to lose it. If you have ever lost control or your composure, if you have ever been pushed beyond your limits, if you have ever had a nervous breakdown, don't be embarrassed. Welcome to the club; everybody loses it sometime. At some point, at some time in some way, everybody loses it. "I thought he was stronger than that." He was stronger than that, ordinarily. But the right tiger came upon him when his strength was not what it normally is. "I didn't think I'd ever see her break." When the right tiger gets a hold of you, anybody will break.

When Elijah ran, he ran to the right place. He ran to Mount Horeb, the mountain of God. He ran to the arms of God. What do we do when we lose it? What do we do when fear overtakes faith? We run to God. There at Mount Horeb God spoke to him not in the night of earthquake, wind, and fire, but in the gentleness, comfort, and communion of the still, small voice. As Elijah felt God's presence in silence, he was able to express his fears and frustrations. He cried, "[Enough is enough. I've had it.] I have been very zealous for the Lord, the God of hosts; for the Israelites have forsaken your covenant, thrown down your altars, and killed your prophets with the sword. I alone am left. [I'm out here fighting this fight by myself.] And they are seeking my life, to take it away" (1 Kings 19:14). Fear will make you feel like giving up sometimes. Sometimes you just get tired of fighting tigers: fighting on the job, fighting in the home, fighting in church, fighting pettiness and jealousy, fighting to make ends meet, fighting your addiction, fighting the devil, fighting your fears. And we say like Elijah, "Enough is enough. I give up. Why try anymore?"

What saved Elijah was that when he panicked and ran, he ran to the Lord. Not to another unfulfilling and unrewarding relationship, but to God. Not to another eating or drinking binge or shopping and spending spree, but to God. What saved Elijah was that when he said "enough," he was talking to God. Not to another human being who was just as confused and had just as many hang-ups as he had, but to God.

The only way I know how to handle tigers in the dark when panic is setting in and I don't know what else to do is to come before God and say, "Father, I stretch my hands to thee; no other help I know. God, here I am, your child. I can't handle these fears anymore. I don't know what else to do. I don't know where to go. I put this fear in your hands. I put myself in your hands. I put these tigers in your hands. You take them because I've had enough."

Now when we go to God in prayer, the fear doesn't leave right away. There was a story of a well-known missionary in India who was bowing one night in prayer at the side of his bed when a great python lowered itself from the rafters of his bungalow and encircled his body with its cold and powerful coils. It made no attempt to constrict, yet the missionary knew that if he struggled, the great serpent would tighten the coils and crush him. With marvelous self-control and courage born of faith, he went on quietly praying, until at length the animal unwound itself and went back into the roof.[4]

Sometimes as we pray, fears will attack us and wrap themselves around us, even as we come before God. That's why we need to learn not only how to pray, but how to pray through. There's a difference in praying and praying through. Praying is talking to the Lord, but praying through is agonizing with the Lord. Praying through means that you continue to pray until the breakthrough comes, until you know you have the victory. When you are trying to overcome a fear, you are engaged in warfare. One battle will not win a war. You keep fighting on your knees over and over again until you feel the fear release its hold and crawl back to wherever it came from. To pray through is to be as determined to get your victory as fear is to overcome you and the devil is to defeat you. To pray through is to say like Jacob when he wrestled with the angel all night long, "I will not let you go. I don't care how long it takes, or how often I have to come to you, or how many setbacks I have or how many tigers are in my cage. I will not let you go until you bless me. I know you can do it. You have the power and you promised never to leave me. Now I'm claiming your promise. I'm going to stay right here until my change comes." That's what it means to pray until you pray through. You pray through sorrow to song; pray through midnight to morning; pray through tears to testimony; pray through weeping to winning.

Elijah prayed through at Mount Horeb and God spoke to him and said:

> Go, return on your way to the wilderness of Damascus; when you arrive, you shall anoint Hazael as king over Aram. Also you shall anoint Jehu son of Nimshi as king over Israel; and you shall anoint Elisha . . . as prophet in your place [and regarding your concern that you are the only one left], I will leave seven thousand in Israel, all the knees that have not bowed to Baal, and every mouth that has not kissed him. (1 Kings 19:15-18)

When you pray through you can face your tigers in the dark. The story is told of a father whose little girl was afraid of the dark. She would call for him in the middle of the night. He would simply stand by her crib and look down upon her. The little girl, knowing that her father was in the room and his eyes were looking down upon her, would fall to sleep peacefully, all fear gone.

You can face your tigers in the dark when you know that beyond them there is another set of eyes watching over you. Even though the tigers can see you better than you can see them, you have no need to fear because the other set of eyes can see every move they make and can move to protect you.

1. James S. Hewett, ed. *Illustrations Unlimited* (Wheaton, Ill.: Tyndall House Publishers, Inc., 1988), no. 3, p. 205.

2. Elan Foster, *6000 Sermon Illustrations* (Grand Rapids: Baker Book House, 1992), no. 2271, p. 271.

3. Clarence E. Macartney, *Macartney's Illustrations* (New York: Abingdon Press, 1946), p. 126.

4. Ibid., p. 77.

Facing Situations You
Have Run From

Text: Exodus 4:18-20

At this point in his life the last thing on Moses' mind, the last thing he ever expected to do, was to go back to Egypt. After all, Moses had run away from Egypt, and when you run away from something, you have no intention of returning. You may move away temporarily, but when you run away, you run away for good. Why did Moses run away from Egypt to begin with when he had everything going for him there? According to Exodus 2:11-15, Moses had killed an Egyptian whom he had seen oppressing a Hebrew. After his crime Moses hid the body in the sand, assuming that no one had seen him. The next day, Moses saw two Hebrews fighting with each other and asked the one who was in the wrong, "Why do you strike your fellow Hebrew?" The man answered him with a question that pierced Moses' heart. He said, "Who made you a ruler and judge over us? Do you mean to kill me as you killed the Egyptian?" Then Moses was afraid and thought, "Surely the thing is known" (Exodus 2:14). The Scriptures further tell us that "when Pharoah heard of it, he sought to kill Moses." Moses ran away because he was a fugitive from justice. We can run away for a number of reasons. We can be a fugitive because of one or more of the five **D's**—**d**epression, **d**isappointment, **d**emons, **d**efeat, or **d**efiance; or one of the four **P's**—**p**ressure, **p**eople, **p**roblems, or **p**rospects; or one or more of the three **F's**—**f**ailure, **f**ear or **f**antasy (the grass always looks greener); or one of the two **M's**—**m**istakes and **m**esses; or the one big **O**—**o**urselves.

One of the enduring lessons of the movie *The Lion King*, however, is that you cannot run away from who you are. When you run from job to job, church to church, and relationship to relationship and have the same problem, maybe the problem is the one who is doing the running.

Moses physically ran away. We may physically try to put some distance or space between ourselves and the source of our irritation. Or we may run away mentally by refusing to face reality or address the situation. We make all kinds of excuses and give all kinds of reasons and tell ourselves all kinds of lies, so that we don't have to deal with the situation. We believe that if we can mentally dismiss a situation, then it will go away.

We can run away emotionally, particularly when we feel physically bound. We tell our heart not to feel, we try to enclose our feelings in a freezer pack of apathy and tell ourselves that we don't care. At least if we can protect our feelings and vulnerabilities, we can put up with what we must without losing our minds and all of our integrity. We then build a world of fantasy to keep our suppressed feelings from being forever stifled.

Some of us run away by becoming workaholics. Others of us do it by becoming overachievers to compensate for our insecurity. Others of us become underachievers because certain things are expected of us. Others become bookaholics, perpetual students always pursuing another career or degree without settling down in any one job or career to apply anything we've learned because that means responsibility. Others of us run away by becoming codependent or emotionally dependent upon others. Others of us run away by becoming blame-aholics, blaming everything that's wrong with us or not right in our lives on somebody else. Some of us run away by becoming misery-aholics: Have you ever met people who are not happy unless they are miserable? Some of us run away by becoming superreligious or spiritual-aholics. Whenever I see people who are holier than thou, who condemn everything they don't like to do or can't do, and who have no sense of humor, I wonder what they are trying to hide or cover up or run away from. Some of us believe that if we have a problem, we can shout it out. Problems cannot be shouted out; they have to be addressed and solved. The emotional release might be therapeutic for us and that's all right as long as we don't expect the problem to go away because we have had a good time in church. A good time in church and an emotional release or the anointing of the spirit do not take away problems, but refresh you, free you, empower you, and prepare you to deal with your problems.

In the text, Moses had not only run away from Egypt but had been away for forty years when God's call came to him to go back. After forty years Moses thought that Egypt was out of his life forever. But God's call to Moses was the wake up call that Moses still had responsibilities in Egypt. Moses still had a job to do in Egypt. The people of God were still being oppressed in Egypt. Taskmasters were still abusing slaves in Egypt. Moses had struck a blow on behalf of one slave. Now he was being charged with striking a blow for many. What Joseph Stalin said about facts also applies to responsibilities: They are "stubborn things." They do not go away simply because we move away and begin another lifestyle. They do not disappear simply because we have a new love or other interests. They do not necessarily fade with time.

If there is a baby in your past, if there is a child in your past, you have a responsibility for that life. A new love, a new life, a new job, a new location, a newfound religion, does not absolve you of your responsibility. If there is unfinished business in your life, you have a responsibility to take care of it. For responsibility is like truth crushed to earth and planted in the soil—it comes up again. Many people, like Moses, believe that certain things are gone from their lives forever—they ran away and got lost. But further on up the road, what they ran away from, at a time and place that they least expected it, stood up and stared them in the face.

When God called Moses, Moses gave all kinds of excuses for not going to Egypt, none of which were acceptable. Things we have run away from will not be put off by excuses when they catch up with us. Moses eventually said, "Send someone else," which was most unacceptable of all because responsibilities have our names upon them and nobody else's. The things we ran away from only we—nobody else—ran away from, and thus nobody else can face them. When certain things track us down, we ask, "How did you find me?" Easy, certain things have only your name on them.

Thus at age eighty Moses found himself returning to a situation that he had fled from. He was directed there by God, who did not send him back to Egypt to fail. Before we return to our respective situations from which we have run we must first seek heaven's direction. Don't undertake the straightening out of a mess or the righting of a wrong without first asking God how to do it. Good intentions are not good enough. Good intentions, the easing of conscience, provide the motivation but they do not give you the road map for the journey or the strategy for either battle or making peace. But whatever heaven directs, heaven blesses. To put the matter succinctly, before you return to something that you ran from, pray before you go.

God told Moses that those who sought his life were now dead. When you pray before you go, the first thing the Spirit reveals is the right time to go. The Lord won't let you go until you are strong enough to face your pharaoh. When God told Moses that those who sought his life were dead, he was telling him that those whom he feared could no longer harm him. Many times we fear things and people who really in and of themselves are no threat. The only power they have is what we give them. The only authority they have is what we give them out of fear. The only control they have is what we allow them to have. Nobody can make you feel inferior; you have to feel inferior on your own. Nobody can make you jealous; you have to decide to be jealous. Nobody can make you hate; you have to hate on your own. Nobody can make you mean and bitter; you have to be mean and bitter on your own. Nobody can make you petty; you have to be petty on your own. Nobody can make you miserable; you have to be miserable on your own. You have to decide to give up control of your emotions and of your mind. Remember that when you are God's child, the only power the devil has over you is what you give up to him. But when you pray before you go, God will direct you when to go and then God will help you put people in their proper perspective. Most importantly, God will help you keep yourself in proper perspective because you will understand that you are not weak but strong.

You are strong because God never sends anyone anywhere without giving that person something to go with. God told Moses to look in his hands. When Moses looked in his hand, his shepherd's rod became a snake. Never forget that what looks ordinary becomes extraordinary in the Lord's hands. Water in the Lord's hands becomes the best wine at the feast, ordinary clay becomes a cure for blindness, a little boy's lunch becomes a banquet for five thousand, and a rugged cross becomes the means of humanity's redemption.

An ordinary preacher's kid in the Lord's hands becomes Malcolm X. A local church pastor in the Lord's hands becomes Martin Luther King Jr., a winner of the Nobel Peace Prize. An ordinary seamstress and stewardess in the Lord's hands becomes Rosa Parks, mother of the modern-day civil rights movement. An ordinary kafir boy in the Lord's hands becomes Nelson Mandela, first black president of South Africa.

Never underestimate what you can do when you are in the Lord's hands. When situations seem impossible, pray for a spirit of discernment, and look in your hands and you will see the strength of Samson and Deborah. Look in your mind and you will see the wisdom of Solomon and Huldah. Look in your imagination and you will see the visions of Joseph and Hagar. Look in your heart and you will see Jesus' capacity to love. Look in your soul and you will feel the strength of your ancestors both in the Bible and out of it who would not be broken by Pharaoh's lash. Look in your hands and you will see the Word of God— believe it. Look in your history and you will see your experience of how the Lord has taken care of you—hold on to it.

God didn't send Moses back to Egypt empty-handed but gave him a rod that became miraculous. When Jacob went to face Esau, God didn't send him empty-handed but gave him herds of cattle to make a peace offering. When God sent Elijah back to Jezebel, God gave him something to go with—the assurance that there were seven thousand more who hadn't bowed knee to Baal. When Jesus sent the disciples back to Jerusalem he gave them something to go with—the promise of a comforter. When Jesus comes back, he's not coming back empty-handed; he is bringing judgment in one hand and rewards for the righteous in the other. So if God sends you, just look in your hands and see what God has given you to go with.

God not only gave Moses a rod, however, but Aaron as an interpreter. In other words, God didn't send Moses by himself. When you follow where God leads you and go where God sends you, you don't go by yourself. And that's the most important question: Is the Lord with us? Sometimes God will allow things to happen we don't understand. God will say no when we want God to say yes or God will say wait when we want God to say now. We can't understand or answer all questions about God and our faith. But there is one answer we must have: Is the Lord with us? We're not worried about Pharaoh's power, we just need to know: Is the Lord with us? We're not worried about obstacles or opposition, or disbelievers and doubters. We just need to know: Is the Lord with us? We can face anything, endure anything, withstand anything, carry and bear up under anything, if we know the answer to this question: Is the Lord with us? We can return to any Egypt and come out again if we know the answer to this question: Is the Lord with us?

If we pray before we go and take what God gives us, we can return in strength to the place we ran from in shame, we can return in faith to the place we ran from in fear, because the Lord is with us. God hasn't brought us this far to leave us. God didn't bring Moses from the rocking of his cradle on the Nile River, to his upbringing in Pharaoh's household, to a forty-year sojourn in the desert to leave him. God didn't bring some of us from the ghettos of the urban north, through the red hills of the deep south, across the dusty plains of the southwest, to leave us now.

God didn't save some of us from a burning hell, raise some of us from sick beds, strengthen some of us to say goodbye to loved ones, help some of us to pay our bills, keep hellhounds and enemies, our foolishness and mistakes from destroying us, to leave us now.

When the devil comes upon us to assault our faith and defeat us, we can tell him, "I don't feel no ways tired. I've come too far from where I started from. Nobody told me the road would be easy. I don't believe God brought me this far to leave me."

Facing Those We Have Hurt

Text: Luke 15:17-19

If you have ever made a mistake, if you have ever gotten off track or off center and out of focus, if you have ever hurt or disappointed or let somebody down, one of the hardest things you will ever have to do is face those whom you have hurt. And essential to our recovery, our redemption, our starting over again is facing those whom we have hurt or disappointed. That's why some people are still in their hog pens. They cannot bear the thought of facing those whom they have hurt. "After what I said or did, after the way I hurt those people or deceived them, how can I look them in the eye again? How can I ask their forgiveness? How dare I ask them a favor? How can I ask them to give me another chance?"

Sometimes before we can go forward, we have to do some backtracking and make some amends, try to clear up some misunderstandings, rebuild some bridges that we have torn down, and try to clean up some of the messes we have made. Anyone who has ever watched anybody work on a house knows that a carpenter, an electrician, or a painter can do only so much work and make so much progress without stopping every now and then to clean up the mess he or she has made. I've noticed over the years that if someone is sloppy about cleaning up, he or she will also do sloppy work. We cannot have a clean future without pausing to clean up some of our messes of the past by trying to fix some of the tattered relationships, broken promises, forsaken friendships, and hearts we have hurt. And if we are sloppy regarding those we have hurt in the past, we will also be sloppy about relationships that we will build in the future.

That was the discovery the prodigal son made in the hog pen when he came to himself. He not only remembered the abundance of his father's house, he also thought about how much he must have hurt his father. The young man knew that where he was would lead nowhere but to more disgrace, more wallowing with the hogs, and death. He realized that before he could get straightened out, he would have to return and face those whom he had hurt. That's the decision that each of us has to make when we have hurt someone. Either stay where we are and be miserable, continue to lose sleep at night, continue to be hypocritical as if the breach we have made doesn't bother us, continue wallowing with the hogs, and die on the vine, or get up and face those we have hurt to see if we can fix what has been messed up.

The prodigal son decided to go back home on a facing and fixing mission. But look at how he goes. Note the speech he has prepared: "Father, I have sinned against heaven and before you; I am no longer worthy to be called your son; treat me like one of your hired hands" (Luke 15:18-19). He went with an humble spirit. He didn't return home with a bitter spirit—"Life has dealt me a rotten hand." He didn't return with a blaming spirit, accusing other folks for his lack of preparation for the "real world." He didn't return with a false spirit, pretending that things were better than they were and he just had a little bad luck. He didn't return with a demanding spirit or an "I'm doing you a favor by returning" spirit.

When he left home he was so sure of himself but when he returned he was humbled. The hog pen will humble you. It's not enough to return, we have to return with the right spirit: a spirit that admits its failures and mistakes rather than one that places blame; a spirit that asks for forgiveness and a second chance rather than one that makes a demand; a spirit that is more concerned with reconciliation than with winning an argument and proving who is right and who is wrong; a spirit that has learned from the hog pen of one's mistakes and has not been made bitter by them. If we don't go back with the right spirit we might as well stay where we are. For the wrong spirit will make things worse rather than better.

The fact that the prodigal son was humbled meant that his pride had been trampled under foot in the hog pen. Don't let pride keep you in the hog pen. Don't let the "what ifs" keep you where you are. Don't let pride stop you from facing and fixing what needs to be confronted and repaired. Pride is keeping many a couple, many a friend, many a family, apart. Pride keeps us in our seat when the invitation is extended to receive Jesus Christ as Lord and Savior by joining the church. Pride is causing some of us to quench the Holy Spirit. What will people think if I join the church after attending here for so long without being a member, if I admit that I need salvation after being a member for so long, or if I shout or stand up and clap? Pride is causing some of us to miss our blessings. Pride is going to send a number of us to hell. Don't let pride keep you where you are. To face those we have hurt means that some of us need to swallow our pride.

In order for the son to think about how much he may have hurt his father shows that this son was sensitive to somebody else's pain besides his own. To face those we have hurt means that we have to be concerned about somebody else's pain, hurt, and heart besides our own. When we make mistakes or when we are harmful to ourselves—our careers, our relationships, and our lives—we not only hurt ourselves, we hurt those who love us. Some people are so wrapped in their own pain that they think they are the only ones hurting. Some people are so busy singing "Woe is me" and "Look at my pain" that they never have time to sing "If I can help somebody." They never have time to say, "I'm hurting, but I know you're hurting too. Let me help you with your pain." Because often when we take the time to help somebody else with his or her pain, we forget about our own for awhile. To face those we have hurt means that we have to stop navel-gazing with self-pity and start looking at others with an eye of compassion. To face those we have hurt, we have to reach a point of maturity at which we realize that we are not the only ones hurting. There is plenty of hurt to go around and not enough healing. So why don't we volunteer to be the one to stand in the gap and say, "I'm going to be the one to help with the healing instead of adding to the hurting." That's what makes Jesus so special: He doesn't come to add to our hurt but to add to our healing. He doesn't come to add to our confusion but to add to our comfort. He doesn't come to add to our damnation but to add to our deliverance.

The younger son began to retrace his steps to his father even though he was in a distant country. The journey back to those we have hurt may be a long one, particularly if time has magnified misunderstanding, eroded truth, distorted perception, and hardened feelings. The road back is always longer and more difficult than we first imagined, but we have to keep walking. Along the way doubts will attack us, second-guessing will slow us down, the "what ifs" will try to block us, but we have to keep walking. Distractions will arise to turn our heads, personal problems will surface from nowhere to trip us, but keep walking. We will notice hills and mountains on our way back that we didn't notice before and sometimes we will wonder if we are lost, but keep walking. For every child of God has a compass. Above us is Jesus, the bright Morning Star. In our hands is the Word of God. David said, "Your word is a lamp to my feet and a light to my path" (Psalm 119:105). Keep walking.

The younger son kept walking, not knowing what awaited him. Lest we forget, the younger son did not know how either the father or the elder brother would receive him. He journeyed without guarantees, and so must we. That's why a number of us are hesitant about facing those we have hurt. We do not know how we will be received. We want a guarantee that people we have hurt will accept us back or be open to hearing us out or at least trying to build new bridges of understanding and communication. "What if I try and they don't receive me or hear me or talk to me? What if I make this long journey and they reject me?"

Well, I wish I could tell you that every time you make an effort to face those you have hurt you will be rewarded and accepted, forgiven and restored, and your efforts to make peace and reach understanding will bear fruit. Sometimes you will make this long journey and those you seek will not be pleased to hear from you, or will see you and still rebuff you. According to the Scriptures the elder brother was not pleased with his younger brother's return. He refused to join the celebration that his father threw to welcome his younger son back home. The elder brother remonstrated with his father:

> "Listen! For all these years I have been working like a slave for you, and I have never disobeyed your command; yet you

have never given me even a young goat so that I might celebrate with my friends. But when this son of yours came back, who has devoured your property with prostitutes, you killed the fatted calf for him." Then the father said to him, "Son, you are always with me, and all that is mine is yours. But we had to celebrate and rejoice, because this brother of yours was dead and has come to life; he was lost and has been found." (Luke 15:29-32)

The parable never tells us that the elder brother and younger brother ever made up. Sometimes when we make the journey back home, we will meet some elder brothers whose hurt is so deep that they cannot welcome us back..

But we must still make the journey. We must make it because our own integrity and redemption depends upon it. Even if the other person rejects us, we need to know before we can make a fresh start that we did try, we did our part, we did our best. Before we can shake the dust from our feet we first have to get them dusty by trying. When we stand before the judgment seat of Christ, we can face him with a clear conscience and tell him that at least we tried. If there is hurt between us and another person, that hurt can weigh both of our souls down. If we try to heal the hurt and the other person rejects our attempt, we may still feel the pain of rejection and lost relationship, but our record is cleared and our soul is free because we tried.

Then, we must make the journey back home, because that's the only way we will find out about the father's love. The focus in the parable is really not only the brother who strayed or the brother who stayed, but the father, whose love was constant. True, there will be some elder brothers who will not receive you, but there will also be some fathers who will welcome you with open arms. There will be some elder brothers who say "away with you," but there will also be some fathers whose love is in abundance and is constant and who will say, "It's celebration time. Get a robe of forgiveness, a ring of love that has no beginning and no end, and shoes of glad tidings for this my daughter, my son, my brother, my sister, my mother, my father, my friend, my companion was dead, but now is alive, lost but now is found." We have to make the journey home because that is the only way we will discover the father's love.

We make the journey home because one day Jesus made a journey to us. He didn't wait until we found our way back to him. He left his Father's house and came to where we were. He had no guarantee that we would receive him, but he came anyhow. When the hogs saw him they tried to destroy him. They crucified him and buried him in the mud. But early Sunday morning he stood up and shook off the mud from the pen and declared "all power." He put the hogs under his feet and reached down and caught our damaged souls and led us from grime to glory.

He's still in the saving business, sanctifying business, lifting business. If you give him a chance he will do it for you.

Facing Weaknesses in
Those We Love

Text: 1 Samuel 25:23-25

None of us is perfect; all of us at some time or another must come to grips with imperfections and weaknesses in those whom we love. The experience of discovering imperfections in the rose that looked so perfect from afar can be disconcerting and discouraging, until we realize that when we get close enough to see the imperfections and weaknesses of others they can also see the imperfections and weaknesses in us. Because our eyes only focus outward and not inward, however, we cannot see ourselves as others see us—we can only see others through our own eyes. So how do we handle the imperfections and weaknesses we see in those we love? The story of Abigail can give us some insight in answering this question.

The incident in the text occurred during that period in David's life when he was roaming the countryside as an outlaw because an insecure and paranoid King Saul had become threatened by David's youth, skills, and popularity and had tried to kill him. David gathered a few men and fled for his life. During his wanderings David and his men had come across some herdsmen who worked for a very wealthy individual whose name was Nabal. David and his men had been very kind to Nabal's herdsmen, providing them protection and doing whatever they could to assist them. During the sheepshearing season, David requested that Nabal give him and his men some food and supplies. David did not make a specific request regarding the amount, but was content to receive whatever Nabal had on hand. David's request would not have been a hardship for Nabal since the sheepshearing season was a time of feasting and celebration. Instead of showing gratitude for the kindness that David and his men had provided for him, Nabal answered David's messengers harshly and curtly. He said: "Who is David? Who is the son of Jesse? There are many servants today who are breaking away from their masters. Shall I take my bread and my water and the meat that I have butchered for my shearers, and give it to men who come from I do not know where?" (1 Samuel 25:10-11). When David received Nabal's reply, he and four hundred armed men prepared to march against Nabal's household.

One of Nabal's servants went to Abigail, however, and told her how well they had been treated by David and his men and how rudely Nabal had been to David's messengers, and that he feared what might befall as a result of his master's insult. When Abigail heard of the incident, she immediately took steps to ameliorate David's wrath. The Bible tells us that she took "two hundred loaves, two skins of wine, five sheep ready dressed, five measures of parched grain, one hundred clusters of raisins, and two hundred cakes of figs" (v. 18). Saying nothing to Nabal, she sent two young men ahead of her and set out to meet David. As he was marching to Nabal's estate, David was saying to himself, "Surely it was in vain have I protected all that this fellow has in the wilderness, so that nothing was missed of all that belonged to him; but he has returned me evil for good. God do so to David and more also, if by morning I leave so much as one male of all who belong to him" (vv. 21-22). It was at this moment that Abigail met David with her gift of generosity. Let me just observe that so often just at the moment when it seems as if our correct living and doing the right thing seem to be for naught, someone comes to us and lets us know that our good deeds have not been in vain. God has a way of encouraging us at just the right moment, just in the nick of time when we are about to give up, so that we will not grow weary in doing right, but understand that in due season we shall reap if we do not faint. Abigail said to David:

> Upon me alone, my lord, be the guilt; please let your servant speak in your ears, and hear the words of your servant. My lord, do not take seriously this ill-natured fellow, Nabal; for

as his name is, so is he; Nabal is his name, and folly is with him; but I, your servant, did not see the young men of my lord, whom you sent. Now then, my lord, as the Lord lives, and as you yourself live, since the Lord has restrained you from blood guilt and from taking vengeance with your own hand, now let your enemies and those who seek to do evil to my lord be like Nabal. And now let this present that your servant has brought to my lord be given to the young men who follow my lord. Please forgive the trespass of your servant; for the Lord will certainly make my lord a sure house, because my lord is fighting the battles of the Lord; and evil shall not be found in you so long as you live. . . . When the Lord has done to my lord according to all the good that he has spoken concerning you, and has appointed you prince over Israel, my lord shall have no cause of guilt or pangs of conscience, for having shed blood without cause or for my lord taking vengeance himself. And when the Lord has dealt well with my lord, then remember your servant. (vv. 24-28, 30-31)

From Abigail's speech we learn several things about facing weaknesses in others. There were five things that Abigail did not do. First, she did not deny that her husband had a problem and that he was a problem. In so many words she said "his name means fool and that's what he is, a fool." Many of us still deny the weaknesses in those we love. Many of us are still trying to pretend that those we love are not as bad off as they are. We seem to feel that love requires us to protect and defend those we love even when they are wrong. But right is right and wrong is wrong and truth is truth. If your loved ones lied, they are wrong. If they started the fight, if they are mean and self-centered, if they are drunk, addicted, if they are lazy or greedy, if they have a gambling or a philandering problem, they are wrong and you do not need to feel obligated by love and loyalty to uphold them in their wrongdoing. Before you get in a huff and curse out somebody about your child, you had better be sure that your child is not in the wrong. Before you jump to somebody's defense and go to war because of what somebody said about your companion, relative, or friend, be sure that your loved one is not in the wrong.

It's never right to uphold wrong even if it is for someone you love. We do not prove our love by making excuses for people who are wrong. Our excuse-making, denial, and protection does not alter the truth that our loved ones are wrong. Our excuses, denials, and attempted cover-ups only make matters worse, not better. We only confirm and encourage our loved ones to stay the way they are until what is wrong gets out of hand. When you see someone whose problem has gotten out of hand, keep in mind it didn't get that way overnight and without someone's help with some covering up and excuse-making. To fix weaknesses in those we love we must first face them and admit that they have a problem.

Second, Abigail did not assume guilt or responsibility for her husband's or loved one's weakness. Sometimes we believe that if we do the right thing, then others will be touched by our goodness and turn from their wicked ways. And when they don't, then we feel guilty because we feel that there is something lacking in our life and love. If we loved a little more, bent over backwards a little more, perhaps they might change. Perhaps they will, but perhaps they won't.

We do the right thing first for our own self and soul's salvation—for we have to die and meet God for ourselves. Then we hope to help others see the light. And sometimes they will, but if they don't we cannot assume responsibility and feel guilty because they don't respond to our good example. I've said it over and over again: people make their own decisions about whom they will serve and the kind of life they choose to live. You cannot assume guilt for somebody else's responsibility. You have enough problems of your own to carry; don't add guilt for what isn't your fault to your load.

And neither can you allow someone to tell you that you are guilty: "I wouldn't be like this if you were a better parent or a better husband or wife or lover or friend or provider." We have to tell people, "You are what you are because you choose to be that way." Abigail did not deny that her loved one had a problem. Abigail did not assume guilt for Nabal's character.

Third, Abigail did not allow her loved one to destroy her. The Bible describes her as intelligent and beautiful. She didn't let Nabal worry her into an early grave, or cause her to become old, shriveled up, and wrinkled before her time. She didn't go off and sit in a corner and neglect her brains and vitality because of his problem. She didn't act dumb or try to hide her beauty because of his insecurities. She didn't let herself go to pieces or her body go to pot because she lived in a difficult situation. She didn't become bitter and mean because she was in a bitter and mean situation or because she was with somebody who was bitter and mean. She was intelligent and beautiful when she met Nabal. She was intelligent and beautiful when she married him. And when he died she was still intelligent and beautiful. Instead of letting Nabal destroy her, Abigail continued to develop.

Don't you dare allow your loved ones to destroy you. Don't you dare give the devil the satisfaction and joy of knowing that he has stolen your joy, defeated you, and gotten the victory over you. I know sometimes that your heart is broken, but don't let heartbreak destroy you. I know somebody who specializes in mending broken hearts. I know sometimes that you have more problems than you can handle. But don't let your problems destroy you. I know somebody who is a problem solver. I know that sometimes your mind is so confused that you don't know which way to turn. Don't let your confused mind destroy you—Jesus is a mind regulator.

You continue to develop. If others act ignorant, you remain intelligent. If others act crazy, you continue to act cultured. If others are wasteful, you continue to show wisdom. If others go backward, you continue to go forward. If others go to hell, you press on toward heaven.

Abigail did not deny her husband had a problem. She did not assume guilt for her loved one's problem. She did not let her loved one destroy her with his problem.

Fourth, she did not stop interceding where she could. That's what she was doing in the text—she was interceding where she could. She could not prevent her loved one from acting up, but she interceded where she could so that his acting up would not mess her up completely. When the devil gets busy you cannot roll over and play dead like a possum or hide your head in the sand like an ostrich or swell up like a blowfish or run around in a circle like a rabbit or change colors like a chameleon or spit poison like a cobra or become hard to handle like a porcupine or roar like a gorilla or run for cover like a squirrel. People who have a problem, if left to themselves, will mess themselves up and you too.

That's what Nabal was about to do. His bad attitude was about to get him killed, all the men who worked for him killed, and the fortune that would have fallen to Abigail destroyed. So

Abigail interceded; she did what she had to do to save the household. Sometimes you don't have time to debate about whose job or responsibility or fault a certain thing is. You just have to do what you have to do to save your family, your future, your faith, your friendships. Sometimes a man or a woman has to do what a man or a woman has to do. Sometimes a mother or a father has to do what a mother or father has to do. Sometimes a son or a daughter has to do what a son or daughter has to do. Sometimes a friend has to do what a friend has to do.

Sometimes even God has to do what God has to do. That's why Jesus came—divine love wrapped in human flesh had to intervene to save us from the shackles of sin, sanctify us for the status of saints, prepare us for a place in paradise, and help us reach the heights of heaven. I'm so glad that when we, by foolishness and callousness, could have caused destruction, grace and compassion intervened and called for our deliverance. And when the devil has my mind so distracted that I cannot even pray right, I'm so glad that the Holy Spirit intervenes with sighs and groans too deep for words and makes my requests known before the mercy seat. Where would we be without the intervention of God the Father, the intercession of Christ the Son, and the interpretation of the blessed Holy Spirit?

Abigail did not deny her loved one had a problem. She did not assume guilt for her loved one's problem. She did not allow her loved one to destroy her. She did not stop interceding where she could. And finally, Abigail did not stop loving and being loyal even though she couldn't save her loved one.

When Abigail told Nabal about her intercession with David on behalf of the household and her generosity, Nabal became so enraged that "his heart died within him; he became like as stone. About ten days later the Lord struck Nabal, and he died" (vv. 37-38). She was a good woman but she had a mean husband that she couldn't save. We cannot save anybody; only Jesus saves. Be careful about believing that if you become connected with someone, you change that person. You cannot change anybody who is not open to change. If someone is not open to being changed, not even God will change that person.

Why keep on loving and why keep on being loyal? Why waste love and loyalty on the Nabals of this world who don't deserve it? The story is told of a young girl who had a large doll collection. In this collection were a number of expensive dolls from all over the world. Some were even rare porcelain dolls dressed in the finest silk. One day a visitor who was looking through the collection asked the young girl which was her favorite. The young girl asked, "Do you really want to know?"

He replied, "Yes, I really do."

The young girl then reached under her bed and pulled out a shoebox. In it was an old rag doll. Its face was smudged and dirty. Some of the hair was missing and the dress was torn and stained. One of the arms was missing and a leg was dangling by a couple of threads. The young girl beamed as she clutched the doll to her chest and said, "This is my favorite doll."

The visitor was surprised and said, "With all of the many finely dressed, perfectly formed, and expensive dolls that you own, why is this rag doll in her condition your favorite?"

"Because," the young girl replied, "I realize that if I don't love her, nobody will."

We love unlovely loved ones who are not worthy of our love because even they need love, and if we don't love them, nobody will. Perhaps that's why God placed us in their lives—because they are still children and they too need love, and if we don't love them perhaps nobody will. Others don't have our personality, our patience, our perseverance.

And when we think about it, that's how God deals with each of us. "In this we know that God loves us, in that while we were yet sinners Christ died for us" (Romans 5:8).

Facing Life after Loss

Text: Luke 24:13-15, 21, 27

At some point in life every one of us will experience some kind of loss. Loss of a blood relative, loss of a friend, loss of a mentor or role model, loss of a spouse, loss of a marriage or relationship, loss of a job, loss of health, loss of sight, hearing, sexual potency, leg, arm, or other body part, loss of mind, loss of faith, and so forth.

Loss is loss. Sometimes we like to "out loss" and "out miserable" each other or debate who had the worst, the greatest, the most devastating loss. "If you think your situation is bad, let me tell you what I've been through." But loss is loss. Never minimize the pain or severity of someone else's loss. What is light stuff to one person can be devastating to another. Someone's loss of hearing can be just as devastating to that person as your loss of a mother or a spouse. Someone's loss of a marriage or relationship can be just as traumatic to that person personally as your loss of a job. For loss is loss.

All loss involves denial, grieving, and anger. All loss requires time to get over it. All loss requires adjustments of our lifestyle. All loss creates a vacuum, an emptiness because something we are accustomed to having in our lives is missing. What is loss? To lose means to L—leave, O—our, S—spirit, E—empty. Loss leaves our spirit empty and creates an aching void that this world cannot fill.

The disciples in our text were attempting to come to grips with a very deep and personal loss. The death of Jesus meant the loss of a teacher and mentor whom they believed in totally, the loss of a friend who stuck closer than a brother. With the death of Jesus some of them lost their sense of purpose and self-identity, because they had identified with him so closely. His death for some meant a loss of faith not only in themselves, but in God. The taunts of their enemies while Jesus was hanging on the cross was still ringing in their ears: "He called on God, let God save him." Some of them couldn't help but ask themselves why God allowed this to happen to their Jesus— their friend, their loved one, their family, their career, their relationship, their life. For these disciples, the death of Jesus meant the loss of a major hope or a major part of what they had believed. Recall their words in verse 21: "We had hoped that he was the one to redeem Israel."

There are several lessons that can be gleaned from these disciples' efforts to face life after loss. Again, recall the text: "Now on that same day two of them were going to a village called Emmaus about seven miles from Jerusalem, and talking with each other about all these things that had happened" (Luke 24:13-14). Two believers were walking together. Two disciples or followers of Jesus Christ were walking together. Part of our coping and recovering ability to face life after loss will depend on the company we keep! When you have experienced loss you don't need to be surrounded by negative people, weak people, petty people, gossiping people, nosy people, those who have nothing more to offer you than a drink, those who have no direction for their own lives, those who will allow you to wallow in self-pity, those who have no hope or help beyond their own resources, those who are full of clichés and pious platitudes that have no meaning and pack no punch.

To face life after loss you need the right company. Find yourself a true believer to walk with, not just a buddy or a church member. Some of the most negative people I know are church members. You don't simply need a fellow member, you need a fellow believer, you need a true follower of Jesus Christ in the body of Christ called church. Find somebody to walk with you who walks with Jesus, who can talk to you about Jesus, and can remind you of the promises of Jesus. Most significantly find somebody who can pray for you and with you. There will be times when you may not be able to pray for yourself. That's when you need somebody to pray for you.

"Now on that same day two of them were going to a village called Emmaus about seven miles from Jerusalem, and talking with each other about all these things that had happened. While they were talking and discussing, Jesus himself came near and went with them" (vv. 13-15). You need to walk with the right company because the right company draws the right company. As those two believers walked and talked together, Jesus joined their conversation. Not an angel, but Jesus himself; not a spirit or a ghost, but Jesus himself. When Jesus joined them he was just keeping a promise: "For where two or three are gathered in my name, I am there among them" (Matthew 18:20).

The promise is that Jesus would be in our midst, not that we would know that he is with us, or that we would see Jesus walking with us. The disciples to whom Jesus appeared did not know that it was Jesus walking with them. To face life after loss we need the company of believers because believers draw the presence of Christ, even though we may not be aware that our Lord is with us. I'm not simply talking about imagining Christ to be with us, I'm talking about the fact that Jesus really is, actually, physically walking with us—we just don't see Jesus or know him.

How can we be sure that Jesus is with us? Because Jesus promised that he would be. If he rose just as he said he would, then Jesus will walk with us just as he said he would. If Jesus promised that if we sought first the kingdom and his righteousness that all things would be given and kept that promise, then he will keep this one. If Jesus promised that demons would be subject to us and kept that promise, then he will keep this one. If Jesus promised that his grace would be sufficient and kept that promise, then he will keep this one. If Jesus promised that prayer would be answered when it is uttered in his name and kept that promise, then he will keep this one. If Jesus promised that heaven and earth would pass away before one word of his would pass away and kept that promise, then he will keep this one. That's why you need a fellow believer to walk with you. Just in case you have forgotten or in case the Adversary has blocked your memory, a fellow believer can remind you of the promises of Jesus.

Well, why doesn't the Lord just reveal himself? Eventually Jesus did in the text, but first he taught the disciples some things from the Scriptures. Eventually we will look back and understand who has been walking with us all along, but first there are some things that we must learn that we can learn only as we walk by faith.

As Jesus walked with the believers, he enlightened their understanding of the Scriptures as he interpreted all the things concerning himself in the Scriptures. To face life after loss, stay in the Word of God, because you find yourself in the Scriptures. If you've ever listened to the devil when you shouldn't have, read about Adam and Eve in Genesis. If you are trying to run from yourself, read about Moses in Exodus. If you have tremendous challenges ahead, read about Joshua in the book of Joshua. If you want assurance that God will give you victory when odds are against you, read about Gideon in the book of Judges.

If you want to see how God gives new life after loss, read about Naomi in the book of Ruth. If you want to see how God will elevate you, read about David in First and Second Samuel. If you want to see how God will bless you when you seek right things, read about Solomon in First Kings. If you want to see the power of one person's prayer, read about Elijah in Second Kings. If you want to see how prayer and study go together, read Ezra. If you want to know about struggles in pursuing a dream, read Nehemiah. If you want to see how God gives victory over enemies, read Esther.

If you want to know about suffering and loss, read Job. If you want to know about praise and paths, read Psalms. If you want everyday wisdom and guidance, read Proverbs and Ecclesiastes. If you want to know the language of love, read Song of Solomon. If you want to know about comfort as well as judgment, read Isaiah. If you want to know how to work through questions of God, read Jeremiah and Lamentations. If you want to know about new life in a valley of dry bones where you are, read Ezekiel. If you want to know how to survive being persecuted for righteousness' sake, read Daniel. If you want to know about love that is long suffering, not abusive, read Hosea. If you want to hear about justice for the poor, read Amos. If you want to see someone trying to run from the word of God, read Jonah. If you want to know how to make it not by power nor by might but by God's spirit, read Zechariah. If you want to know how to do the journey from a doubt to a shout, read Habakkuk. If you want to learn about tithing, read Malachi.

If you want to know who Jesus is and what he will do for you, read Matthew, Mark, Luke, and John. If you want to know how the Holy Spirit will work in your life, read Acts. If you want clarification of what we believe, read Romans. If you want to know about the resurrection of the body, read First Corinthians. If you want to know about becoming a new creature in Christ Jesus, read Second Corinthians. If you want to know how social distinctions between race and sex are dissolved in Christ Jesus, read Galatians. If you want to know about the whole armor of God, read Philippians. If you want to know about being risen with Christ, read Colossians. If you want to learn of the second coming, read First and Second Thessalonians. If you want to know how to endure hardship as a good soldier, read Second Timothy. If you want to know about faith, read Hebrews. If you want to know how to balance works and faith, read James. If you want to learn about redemption by the precious blood of Jesus, read First Peter. If you want to know about love of God and the love we ought have for one another, read First John. If you need to be reminded that God will keep you from falling, read Jude. If you desire the assurance that when it's all over, evil will be vanquished and victory will be yours because he—our Alpha and Omega who is faithful and true, King of kings and Lord of lords—will bring it, read Revelation.

To face life after loss, stay in the Word of God.

Facing Life after Heartbreak

Text: John 4:16-19, 28-30

The time of day was noon and she had come to the well to draw water. But why was she at the well at noon when the usual time to draw water was early in the morning and early in the evening, in the cool of the day? That's when the other women came. Perhaps that is the very reason that this woman was coming at noon: to avoid the other women, the stares, the whisperings, the cattiness, coldness, and meanness from the old village women, some of whom were probably very religious. This particular woman was not like the other village women. She had been involved in a series of relationships, all of which had ended in heartbreak, hurt, disappointment, disaster, and divorce.

She came to the well by herself because she was a victim of double pain. She had pain in her heart and pain from a community that judged her, talked about her, didn't understand her, and just stayed in her business. She came to the well by herself because she had mess in her life. Heartbreak and breakups can mess with you. They can mess with your head and give you a self-esteem problem. They can cause you to doubt yourself as a man or a woman, lover, friend, companion, particularly when you see other relationships that seem to be happy and making it. Heartbreak and breakups can cause you to feel inferior to others or self-conscious, particularly when others are self-righteous, condemning, and arrogant about the lifestyle of a single person. I have lived long enough to discover that sometimes married people are so hard on some single people not because they have it all together but because they are envious, insecure, and threatened by the freedom of those who are single. In their heart of hearts they are really not that happy and want to be free themselves, but cannot be because they feel trapped.

Heartbreak and breakup can not only mess with our head, they can mess with our heart and make us overly cautious, suspicious, protective, and paranoid about loving again, lest we be hurt again. After heartbreak we ought to be cautious, wiser, but not paranoid. Heartbreaks, if we let them, will also mess with our spirits and cause us to be bitter. You can recognize a bitter person. A bitter person extols and expounds the "all men are dogs" philosophy or the "women cannot be trusted because they'll take everything you have" attitude.

How do we face life after heartbreak and breakup? Everyone, including those most happily yoked, has some heartbreak. How do we fix a broken heart? The first step toward recovering from heartbreak is to get on with the rest of your life as best you can. The Samaritan woman in our text did not allow her repeated heartbreaks and breakups to stop her from functioning. She did not become catatonic and go off in a corner and wither up and die. She continued to live, function, and survive as best she could. By this time she understood all too well that in the final analysis, nobody was going to look out for herself but her. And so she did the best she could to make it from day to day. Though lonely at times, she was still making it. Though in pain a lot of the time, she was still making it. Though misunderstood and talked about much of the time, she was still making it.

She knew that whenever she left the house she might run into one of the good gossiping sisters or one of the crass community brothers. She had a choice, however. She could either shut herself up in her house and die, or she could face the world and do what she needed to do. She adjusted her schedule for going to the well to avoid the confrontations she could, but she didn't stop going to the well. Life for her had to go on and so she did what was necessary to survive.

How do we face life after heartbreak? By facing it. Life has to go on. Life may be different or lonely or painful, but we still must keep on living. For, when we stop to think about it, life wasn't perfect when we were in a relationship. If it had been we wouldn't be trying to handle our heartbreak. We had problems in the relationships and we have problems after the relationships. Either way we're going to have problems, so we might as well decide to be victorious over our new set of problems.

One day this Samaritan woman came to the well with her messy past and met the Messiah, Jesus Christ, the Anointed of God. They began to talk. They talked about the prejudice that had existed between Jesus and his people, Galilean and Judean Jews, and her people, the Samaritans. They talked about the nature of worship. When we really read the fourth chapter of John, we discover that this Samaritan woman and Jesus were engaged in a heavy theological discussion. Others looked at her and would not expect such a conversation from her. Her conversation with Jesus indicated that this much maligned woman had a vibrant mind that she wasn't afraid to use. If we would fix a broken heart, we must remember that we still have a mind. Don't be afraid to use it for something other than self-pity. If your mind can come up with something to complain about, it can also come up with something to give praise for. If your mind can come up with excuses for not doing, then it can come up with reasons for doing.

In the course of the conversation Jesus asked the woman about her present relationship and in so doing she discovered that he knew her. Even though Jesus didn't approve of her present life, neither did he reject her. If our broken hearts are to be fixed then we must understand that Jesus knows and understands how we feel. "Nobody knows," you say. I say, "You're wrong." Jesus knows all about our troubles. He knows about rejection. Jesus' own people in Nazareth rejected him. Jesus knows what it is to be misunderstood by those closest to you. His own brothers and sisters thought he was crazy. Jesus knows what it is to be regarded with suspicion. The religious leaders of his day looked upon Jesus with suspicion. Jesus would one day know betrayal and denial. He would know agony as he prayed in Gethsemane. Jesus would know loneliness like never before when he hung out on a cross to die for your sins and mine.

What I am saying is that we must never forget that we are not alone. No single person who knows Jesus is ever alone. We may not see Jesus but he is there. We may not see air but we know it's there because we're breathing. We may not see our heart beating, but we know it's there and it's working because we're still alive. We may not see the mechanism of the ear at work, but we know that it is functioning because we can hear. We may not see the nerve endings under our skin, but we know they are there because we can still feel. And when dark clouds come, we may not see the sun but we know it's there, because if it wasn't life would disappear from the earth.

So as we face life after heartbreak we must remember that life goes on, that we still have a mind, that Jesus understands how we feel and that we are never alone, and that Jesus loves us even when we make mistakes. This Samaritan woman was involved in a relationship that she should not have been involved in. Sometimes we make mistakes in judgment. Sometimes in our efforts to cope with our loneliness and pain we do things we shouldn't, we become involved in things we shouldn't. Jesus confronts us about those. But he doesn't reject us. He doesn't write us off as hopeless or evil or wicked. He loves us anyway.

After her conversation with Jesus the Samaritan women ran into the village declaring, "Come and see a man who told me everything I have ever done!" Is this the same woman who came to the well at noon to avoid others, now running into the town as a used-to-be nobody telling everybody about somebody who can save anybody? My point here is simple—if we allow Jesus to work on us and in us, he will give us a new love and a new life, a new message and new meaning, new purpose and new power, a new demeanor and new deliverance, new convictions and new compassion, new fire and new freedom, new salvation and new somebodiness, new promise and new praise, new beauty and new boldness, new testimony and new transformation, new righteousness and new resurrection, new glory and new grace, a new witness and a new work, new healing and new holiness, new sanctification and new soul satisfaction, a new song and new strength, a new majesty and a new magnetism, a new smile and new sainthood, a new vision and a new victory.

The woman at the well discovered that Jesus had a word for her. To face life after heartbreak we must understand that Jesus has a word for us: "Come to me all you that are weary and are carrying heavy burdens, and I will give you rest. Take my yoke upon you, and learn from me; for I am gentle and humble in heart, and you will find rest for your souls" (Matthew 11:29-30).

Jesus has a word for us: "You must be born again" (John 3:3).

Jesus has a word for us: "I came that they may have life, and have it abundantly" (John 10:10). Jesus has a word for us: "Blessed are those who mourn, for they will be comforted" (Matthew 5:4). Jesus has a word for us: "I am standing at the door, knocking; if you hear my voice and open the door, I will come in to you and eat with you, and you with me" (Revelation 3:20).

Jesus has a word for us: "Everyone who drinks of this water will be thirsty again, but those who drink of the water that I will give them will never be thirsty. The water that I give will become in them a spring of water gushing up to eternal life" (John 4:13-14).

Facing Life When the Glory Has Gone

Text: 1 Samuel 4:21-22

The incident in our text comes from a period of fear and frustration, tenuousness and tension, difficulty and disappointment, darkness and dread in the life of the people of God called Israel. The Ark of the Covenant, one of Israel's most precious and respected symbols, had fallen into enemy hands. The Ark of the Covenant was essentially a chest that held replicas of the tablets that Moses had received on Mount Sinai when God gave him the Ten Commandments. Some believed that it also contained the rod of Moses. The Ark of the Covenant represented the very presence of God among God's people. The people of Israel had such faith in the Ark that they sometimes carried it into battle believing that as they did, God was with them and therefore they could not be defeated.

This was what happened in the text: The Israelites had carried the Ark of the Covenant into one of their battles against the Philistines. When the Philistines recognized the Ark's presence among the Israelites, they fought much harder against the people of God. The only way to defeat the devil, the ancient Philistine enemy and adversary of our soul, is by defeating the devil. Not debating with him, playing with him, catering to him, trying to avoid him, not hoping he will leave you alone, not throwing yourself on his mercy, but by beating him. The devil will not turn tail and run just because we join the church or because we become more prayerful or more spiritual. Increased spirituality means that the devil will war against us all the more.

Even though the devil knows that his end is destruction he will fight until the end because some of the devil's most prized souls were those that he corrupted at the end. Solomon was a wise and devoted king, but in his latter days he allowed his heart to be turned away from God. Judas was one of Jesus' most trusted disciples, but Satan got him at the end. Ananias and Sapphira were two of the church's leading members, but Satan got them at the end.

The Philistines redoubled their fighting efforts and this time they won the battle and captured the Ark of the Covenant. When the devil redoubles his efforts we must redouble ours. We cannot rely on what we have done, how we have served or prayed or worked or worshiped, to sustain us when the devil redoubles his efforts. A Sunday morning worship, a ten-minute prayer in the morning, a chapter or two from the Bible everyday, may sustain us during normal times, but not when the devil has turned up the heat and has sent for reinforcements. We must increase in prayer, as he increases in ploys. We must increase in the Word, as he increases in his wiles. We must increase in determination as he increases in deviousness. We must increase in faith as he increases his fight. We must increase in getting up as he increases in tripping us up.

And there will be times when the devil will get the best of us. Read the Scriptures and you will discover that at some point the devil got the best of the strongest and the best; the Bible tells us that at some point on their faith journey, Abraham, father of the faith, doubted and lied; Moses lost his temper; David plotted the death of one of his most conscientious followers; Elijah panicked, ran, and asked God to take his life; Esther was hesitant about interceding for her people; Jeremiah decided not to preach anymore; John the Baptist questioned whether Jesus was really the Messiah; Simon Peter denied his friendship with the Lord; and in Gethsemane even Jesus agonized in prayer: "My Father, if it is possible, let this cup pass from me"(Luke 22:42).

Life is not some straight uphill journey from sinner to saint, from hell to heaven, from addict or abuser to angel. Rather life is a winding road with ups and downs. Sometimes we get the best of the devil and life is full of glory. And sometimes the devil gets the best of us and life loses its glory. How do we face life when life has lost its glory?

In the text, when the Ark of the Covenant was captured, the

news was carried to Eli, the old priest who had cared for it. The tragic news from the battle was too much for the old man. Not only was the Ark captured but Eli's two sons Hophni and Phinehas were also killed in battle. Eli was able to withstand the news of the death of his sons, but when he was told of the Ark's capture he fell backwards from his chair and broke his neck and died. Eli's son Phinehas had a pregnant wife who was near the time of delivery.

When she heard the news that the Ark of God was captured, and that her father-in-law and her husband were dead, she bowed and gave birth, for her labor pains overwhelmed her. As she was about to die, the women attending her said to her, "Do not be afraid, for you have borne a son." But she did not answer or give heed. She named the child Ichabod, meaning "The glory has departed from Israel," because the Ark of God had been captured and because of her father-in-law and her husband. She said, "The glory has departed from Israel, for the Ark of God has been captured" (1 Samuel 4:19-22).

Today some mother or father knows how the wife of Phinehas must have felt. For them the glory of having children has gone as those children have done some things to break their hearts. Today glory has gone for some woman or man who wished for a child and didn't have one, and may never have one. Today glory has gone for a husband or wife or lover whose relationship didn't work out. Today glory has gone for some worker or professional whose career never amounted to what that person thought it would. Today glory has gone for that young person who didn't make the team, didn't win the prize, or was not accepted by the group. Today glory has gone for some senior who feels that life has passed him or her by. Today glory has gone for somebody who had a dream that seems unreachable when that person looks at the hurdles that still must be overcome. Today glory has gone for somebody whose health is under attack from sickness and disease. Today glory has gone for someone who has had to say goodbye to a loved one. Today glory has gone for some saint for whom the church has lost its thrill.

If you are one of those for whom the glory has gone or if the devil has ever gotten the best of you, there is a word from the Lord that I have for you. That word is this: the glory may be gone but love, hope, joy, peace, power, and perseverance can linger on. Phinehas's wife made one mistake—she equated the Ark of the Covenant, which represented the presence of God, with the very God that the Ark only represented. The Ark may have been captured, but God wasn't captured. The Ark may have been in enemy hands, but God's presence never left God's people.

That's what we must always remember when the devil captures our children, our loved ones, our dreams. All is not over because God still lives. Sometimes the devil will capture our symbols, but he can't touch our Savior. Sometimes we will lose a battle, but the blood of Jesus still prevails. As a preacher I'm acutely aware that sometimes he will corrupt the institutional church, but he cannot corrupt Christ. And sometimes preachers will mess up, but the prayers of the righteous avail much. Sometimes church members will fail you, but Christ's promises are always kept. Don't you dare lose your hope, or give up on your dreams, or assume that a lost battle means a lost war, or a setback means permanent failure—not as long as God lives to answer prayer, work miracles, and make ways out of no way. Remember, God can restore what the devil captured.

As the wife of Phinehas died believing the glory had departed, so one day a king whose name was David would dance in the streets of Jerusalem because he was bringing the Ark of the Covenant back home. As there are some here today for whom the glory has departed there are others who can testify that glory can return because God can restore what the devil took. God can restore glory. God can restore children, a life, companions, faith, joy, love, peace, and power that the devil took. Before you give up altogether remember that God is still in the resurrecting, restoring, reviving, renewing, reestablishing, and recreating business.

Not only can God restore what the devil captured, God can give you new glory. Centuries later an angel appeared to an humble maiden and told her she would bear a son. Even though no prophet had arisen in the land for over four hundred years, and even though God's people were being oppressed by one of history's strongest powers, the Roman Empire, this child was not to be named Ichabod, meaning the glory had departed. For God was about to do a new thing. So the child was to be named Jesus, for he would save his people from their sins.

By that time the Ark of the Covenant had been lost for

centuries. But God had planned another symbol to eternally remind us that not only will God restore what the devil took but God will bathe it with new glory. For God took the same cross that the devil used to capture Jesus and gave it new glory. When Jesus arose after his crucifixion he became our eternal reminder that God not only restores but gives new glory. Maybe you have made some mistakes and let some opportunities pass you by. God will not turn back the clock, but God will give what you have left, the life you have left, the time you have left—new glory.

Perhaps the devil has messed up and messed with your dreams. God can still bestow new glory out of every setback and disappointment. Out of every trial and tribulation, look for new glory. Therefore as you grow older, don't regret youth that cannot be recovered, look for new glory. Paul reminds us, "For we know that if the earthly tent we live in is destroyed, we have a building from God, a house not made with hands, eternal in the heavens" (2 Corinthians 5:1). And when all seems lost, hold up the cross as God's eternal symbol of new glory.

Facing Persecution When You Are Doing the Right Thing

Text: Daniel 3:16-18

One of the most frustrating experiences believers encounter occurs when we find ourselves being persecuted, ostracized, in trouble, or suffering when we are trying to do the right thing. We can't help but ask, "Why?" After all, if we are doing the right thing, God ought to make our lot easier than what it is and shield or protect us from those who would do us harm. Why are the evil allowed to give the good so much hell? I cannot and would not even dare to try to answer all of the questions about the suffering of the righteous at the hands of the wicked. But there are several things I would suggest you remember when you have to face persecution for doing the right thing.

First, when you stand for the right thing there will be things you naturally are against and people you naturally oppose based upon who you are, what you believe in, and what you stand for. The Nebuchadnezzars of our lives still build monuments to their limited and temporary power. They demand that if you love them, are loyal to them, want to get along with them, or be their friend, or if you want to advance your career or save your job or your benefits, then you must bow down and worship them, sleep with them, kiss up to them, or support them in what you know is wrong. If you have standards or convictions about what is right or wrong, if your soul and your integrity mean something to you, if your self-respect is not negotiable, if your faith and your religion have said to you "this far and no farther," then some things you will be against and some people you will oppose. Life will demand that you take a stand and make choices about what you will live for and what you will fall for. You cannot simply mind your own business, try to get along with everybody, hope that people will respect what you believe and leave you alone and let you get by with a trouble-free existence or a minimum of interference.

Everyday life will demand that we take stands. Everyday life and the devil will test us to see how far they can push us, how much we will bend, if we will break, and how much we are willing to take. When there is moral warfare going on, when there is warfare for the souls of men and women, boys and girls, there are no safe and secure positions of neutrality. You either have to vote yes or no—abstentions not allowed. At some point we have to take a stand.

When you decide to take a stand on anything you will discover two things. First, as I have stated, stands by their very nature mean that some things and people you "ain't for." To stand for something is to stand against some things. Some ask, "Why can't we all just get along?" Because we ain't all for the same things. Second, when we take a stand we discover that there are consequences for our taking a stand. In today's text Nebuchadnezzar found out that Shadrach, Meshach, and Abednego refused to worship Nebuchadnezzar's god not because he observed them himself but because others who were doing the bowing told on them. They had seen how Shadrach, Meshach, and Abednego were advancing and resented them for being blessed as they were. And so instead of trying to learn the secret of their success and emulate it—that would have been the right thing—they chose to try to destroy them.

When you do right, God will bless you. God will prepare a table for you in the presence of your enemies. And people will resent your being blessed. So instead of watching what you do and trying to emulate it, they choose to persecute you. Instead of trying to tithe as you do and instead of actively serving the Lord as you do, they choose to lie on you. Instead of saying "Praise God" and "Thank you, Jesus" as you do, rather than "Look at what I did" like they do, they choose to undermine you. Instead of taking time to come to church because God's Word tells us to "forsake not the assembling of the saints," they choose to plot against you. Instead of seeking God's will first, in prayer and the studying of God's Word—as you do—they choose to report you to Nebuchadnezzar.

You wonder why you are being persecuted when you stand for right. Some people resent your being blessed as you are. People only resent you when you have something or have something going for you, and are prospering in ways that they cannot understand. So if you are being persecuted when you are doing right, that's a sign that you are being blessed and the demons are frustrated. Demons wouldn't be after you if you didn't have something that they didn't have. The only way a demon is going to like you is when you don't have anything or when you're suffering. With every blessing from God, demons will hit at you. I'd rather have the Lord's blessings and a demon's anger, instead of a demon's approval while the Lord withdraws the Lord's blessing hand. I don't know about you, but I've decided demons can get as angry as they want, swell up with jealousy as much as they want, spread as many lies and rumors as they want— I'm going to enjoy my blessings. For if you are doing the right thing, demons cannot stop God's blessings from coming your way. When they close one door, God will open up another.

When Shadrach, Meshach, and Abednego stood for the right they were persecuted by a king who did something they were obligated to oppose, and by others who were jealous of their blessings. But let us observe their answer to their persecutors:

> O Nebuchadnezzar, we have no need to present a defense to you in this matter. If our God whom we serve is able to deliver us from the furnace of blazing fire and out of your hand, O king, let him deliver us. But if not, be it known to you, O king, that we will not serve your gods and we will not worship the golden statue that you have set up. (Daniel 3:16-18)

Their answer indicated two things. First, an unswerving faith in what they knew was right, no matter what the consequences. When facing persecution for doing right you have to be prepared to go all the way with right. Like Job, you have to be prepared to say, "Though he slay me, yet shall I trust him." Right is the right thing to do not because you will always win. Right is the right thing to do because it is right.

Their answer revealed that they were prepared to do some

furnace time. Every great soul who has ever amounted to anything or done anything worthwhile has had to spend some time in the furnace. Sometimes the furnace is physical as it was for Shadrach, Meshach, and Abednego, or as it was with the apostle Paul who had a physical thorn in his flesh. Sometimes, like Joseph, jealousy will sell us out and lies will imprison us, but every life does some furnace time. Sometimes the furnace takes the form of death of loved ones as it did with Naomi, but everybody has some furnace time. Sometimes, like Jeremiah, we find ourselves being lowered into a pit of despair, but every life has to spend some time in the furnace. Sometimes, like Job, we may lose health and wealth, we may lose everything we've acquired and have to start all over again, but every life has to spend some time in the furnace. Sometimes, like Daniel, we may find ourselves in a lion's den surrounded by enemies, but every life has to spend some time in the furnace. Sometimes, like David, we may find ourselves falsely accused by insecure people who hound us day after day and week after week, but every life has to spend some time in the furnace. Sometimes, like John the Baptist, we may find ourselves wondering if our living is in vain when the place we find ourselves after standing for right begins to close in upon us, but every life has to spend some time in the furnace. Sometimes, like Jesus on Calvary, we may find ourselves not only crucified but buried, but every life has to spend some time in the furnace. So when things get really hot for you, just know that it's furnace time. *It's furnace time.*

What was God's response to Shadrach, Meshach, and Abednego's stand? When sufficient time was spent in the furnace, Nebuchadnezzar rushed in to behold the fate of Shadrach, Meshach, and Abednego. I imagine that he stared hard, blinked, and looked again. Then he turned to his counselors in disbelief and asked, "Was it not three men that we threw bound into the fire?"

They answered the king, "True, O king." He replied, "But I see four men unbound, walking in the middle of the fire, and they are not hurt; and the fourth has the appearance of a god" (Daniel 3:24-25).

That is why right is worth standing for, because when you stand for right, you do not stand by yourself, God stands with you. Jesus, the captain of the Lord's host, fights with you, and the Holy Spirit is like wind in your furnace.

Note that Nebuchadnezzar saw the person walking with them. It doesn't say that Shadrach, Meshach, and Abednego saw their visitor or that their visitor said anything to them. Sometimes when you are in the furnace, you may not see God or hear God speak, but God is still with you. How do you know? Because you are surviving in a furnace that was supposed to destroy you. You're walking around in the traps where enemies thought they had you bound. You're walking through that mess that was supposed to stop you. You're walking through those lies that were supposed to discredit you. You're being blessed in the very fire that should have consumed you.

Shadrach, Meshach, and Abednego walked out of the furnace. Jesus got up out of the grave. Nelson Mandela walked out of his prison, but John the Baptist was beheaded and Martin Luther King Jr. died in his Memphis furnace. Sometimes you may not always physically walk out of your furnace, but God is still with you. Remember Dr. King's testimony in the midst of his furnace: "I've been to the mountaintop . . ."

The writer of Hebrews gave this testimony:

> All these died in faith without having received the promises, but from a distance they saw and greeted them. They confessed that they were strangers and foreigners on earth, for people who speak in this way make it clear they are seeking a homeland. . . . But as it is, they desire a better country, that is a heavenly one. Therefore God is not ashamed to be called their God; indeed, he has prepared a city for them. (Hebrews 11:13)

Facing Public Embarrassment

Text: John 8:3-5

What was your moment of public embarrassment? Was it a career crisis? Was it a divorce you didn't think would ever happen to you? Was it something that involved your family? Your daughter became pregnant out of wedlock or your son got somebody pregnant? Did you embarrass yourself or did somebody you love embarrass you because of drunkenness or drugs? Did your companion or friend publicly embarrass you? Did somebody you had faith in betray you and make you feel like a fool? Did something push you too far and for a moment you lost it and said some things and did some things that surprised even you? How you wish you could erase those five or ten minutes when you lost it. Did that secret that you have been hiding get out? Was it the time you were rejected, mocked, and ridiculed by a certain group? Were you or are you involved in some kind of scandal?

Well, if you have ever had a moment of public embarrassment then you ought to be able to empathize with the woman in the text. No one is excusing her behavior. The issue we are focusing on is how humiliating it must feel to have all of her dirty linen aired in public. Before we self-righteously declare that she is getting what she deserved—after all, she did wrong—I would remind you that all of us have done some wrong and but for the grace of God, there go we. All of us have done some things and said some things in private that we would find humiliating if they got out.

Well, if you have ever had a moment of public embarrassment, one of the first things you will discover is that there will always be an audience ready to receive the worst news and run with it. Sometimes we as humans act like vultures swooping down on a dead carcass, the way we pounce on anything and anybody whenever there is the slightest trace of impropriety and scandal.

As short as life is, as fleeting as time is, as many problems as you have in your own life, as short as your money is, with all that you need to do and could be doing, why are you wasting your precious time and energy on somebody else's personal troubles?

If you have ever had a moment of public embarrassment, you will not only discover an audience ready to receive the worst, but that audience will not be quite right themselves. Listen to their charge: "Teacher, this woman was caught in the very act of committing adultery. Now according to the law . . ." (John 8: 4). They didn't say that she was caught right after she finished but in the very act. You cannot commit adultery by yourself. You have to commit adultery with someone. Thus to be caught in the very act of committing adultery, she had to be caught with someone. Where was the someone she was caught with? To be more specific, adultery involves a man and a woman. Two men and two women cannot commit adultery. Adultery means that one or both people involved is married. Two men and two women cannot be married. Marriage is a union ordained and established by God between a man and a woman. So because the charge is adultery, where was the man that the woman was caught with? Moses' law demanded that both, not one, be stoned.

The scribes and the Pharisees brought the woman, and they were all men. Could this case be another example of a form of self-righteous hypocrisy in which men cover up for men and make the woman the scapegoat? Could this be another instance of the rich and powerful covering up for the rich and powerful, while the poor and defenseless are made accountable to the law? In this country, rich gentlemen farmers are paid big bucks not to grow food and are protected by the law. And yet a welfare mother who gets a little extra from the system is painted as a villain and made the scapegoat for the country's deficit.

If you ever have a moment of public embarrassment, before

you allow others to make you feel worthless, look at those doing the most talking, making the most noise and accusations, holding the biggest rocks. They are not exactly perfect themselves. They are not telling the whole truth about themselves. Perhaps the reason they are so hard on you is that you remind them of their own shortcomings. Or perhaps they are trying to cover up something and pointing at you lessens their chances of exposure. If they can keep the spotlight on you, if they can keep people talking about you, folk won't be paying too much attention to them. If we can talk about what somebody is doing or is not doing, somebody won't notice what we are or are not doing.

The enemies of this woman made one mistake, which was also her salvation: They brought her to Jesus. Do you have public shame? Are you feeling that you will never recover from your mistake, from what happened? Have you ever felt that you could not face the public or face people again? I recommend Jesus. Bring your shame, your guilt, your wounded heart, your hurt, your embarrassment, your fear, your damaged self-worth to Jesus.

Do you have people working on you "24, 7, 365?" Do you have people casting your name out as evil, and saying vicious and cruel things about you, spreading your business in the street? Bring them to Jesus. Don't try to handle them yourself; they are beyond your control. You cannot stop people from talking about you. No matter how many hoops you jump through, you cannot stop people from talking. No matter how many tears you shed, you cannot stop people from talking. As a matter of fact, the more you cry and the weaker people perceive you, the more they talk. The more you take, the more some people will dump on you.

So what do you do? You bring yourself and you bring your accusers to Jesus. That's what the writer of the hymn was talking about when he said: "I must tell Jesus all of my trials. I cannot bear these burdens alone. In my distress he kindly will help me, he ever loves and cares for his own."

Let others talk on the phone; you talk in prayer. Let others talk in public; you talk in private. Let others talk on their feet; you talk on your knees. Let others talk to each other; you talk to the Lord:

Here I am Lord, your child. I know I've made my mistakes,

but I'm still your child. Have mercy, Lord. The mockers and scoffers, doubters and knockers, faultfinders and false accusers, the gossipers and self-righteous tale carriers and busybodies are all around me. I don't know what to do. I can't stand up to them by myself, but I know I'm your child. And, I know you're able to bring me through. So I'm putting myself and them in your hands, and I'm asking for deliverance, in the name of Jesus.

If in your moment of public embarrassment you turn to the Lord, the Lord will do two things. First, he will take care of your accusers. According to the Scriptures,

> Jesus bent down and wrote with his finger on the ground. When they kept on questioning him, he straightened up and said to them, "Let anyone among you who is without sin be the first to throw a stone at her." And once again he bent down and wrote on the ground. When they heard it, they went away, one by one, beginning with the elders; and Jesus was left alone with the woman standing before him. (John 8:6-9)

He didn't strike anybody dead, give anybody bad luck, or cause anybody or their family to get sick. He just silenced her accusers and got them away from her. One by one, they tiptoed away. The Lord has his own way of dealing with people. He doesn't necessarily cause anything bad to happen to them. He just has a way of making them harmless. We want the Lord to hurt them, but often the Lord just makes them harmless. That's all we need. The lions that Daniel faced were still lions, the Lord just made them harmless for Daniel. The fire that the three Hebrew boys faced could still burn, the Lord just made it harmless for them. Patmos was still a place of banishment, but the Lord just made it harmless for John. Prison was still a place of punishment, but the Lord just made it harmless for Paul and Silas. Calvary was still a place of disgrace, but the Lord just made it harmless for Jesus. Death is still death, but the Lord just made it harmless for a Christian. "O death, where is thy sting? O grave, where is the victory?" (1 Corinthians 15:55). Accusers will still be accusers, but the Lord will make them harmless to you.

Then, after Jesus handles accusers, he has a word of healing and hope, faith and a future, intercession and inspiration, compassion and confirmation, deliverance and direction, mercy and meaning for us. Jesus asked the woman, "Where are your accusers"? She replied, "I don't know where they are Lord. They were here a while ago. They were causing me to shed tears and lose sleep a while ago. But they don't seem to bother me anymore." Jesus said, "Neither do I condemn you. Go your way and from now on do not sin again."

In other words, you have another chance. Learn your lesson and keep on going. Don't look back, because you have a new future. Hold your head up and be about your business.

If you come to Jesus, then some way, somehow, he will help you pull yourself together and keep on living. Yes, he will, I'm a witness that he will. You will be able to testify like the writer:

Trouble in my way, I gotta cry sometimes
Trouble in my way, I gotta cry sometimes
I stay awake at night, but that's alright
I know Jesus will fix it afterwhile.[1]

My mind is made up
I'm on my way up
I'm gonna hold my head up
Going on with the Lord.[2]

---

1. "Trouble in My Way," p.d.
2. "My Mind Is Made Up," p.d.

Facing the Untouchable

Text: Mark 1:40-42

The text records two very bold actions. The first bold move was made by the leper who approached Jesus begging for healing. This action by the leper was bold because in the time of Jesus, lepers were not only considered unclean but untouchable. Anything they touched was burned, and any people they touched became tainted and had to separate themselves from the community until they were purified. Because lepers were untouchable, they lived in separate communities and whenever they came around people they had to yell "unclean" so that individuals in the immediate area could flee from their presence. If lepers were spotted, people often threw stones at them to make sure they kept their distance. Because both the origin and cure of leprosy were unknown, and because it was believed to be contagious, the skin-dissolving and bone-consuming disease known as leprosy was the most repugnant, most dreaded, and most feared disease in ancient times.

Thus, in the text, when the leper ventured forth in public to find and approach Jesus, he was making a bold move. Where did he get such boldness? Perhaps his was a boldness born of desperation that can make you daring. If you get desperate enough, you will do things you wouldn't do ordinarily. Be careful about saying what you will never do; you never know how desperate circumstances of life will make you. Leprosy is the kind of illness that will drive one to desperation not only because of what it does to one externally but internally as well. To have a disease that eats away at your limbs and makes you loathsome to look at is bad enough. But then to live with the loneliness that this disease brings as humans withdraw from you and treat you worse than a street dog is enough to kill the spirit as well. Any physical disease can be borne, if one's spirit is alive and fighting. But when the spirit, the self-worth of a person is undermined and attacked, and there is no human comfort, compassion, and understanding except from fellow sufferers who are living with their own pain and problems, and there is no escape but death, then one begins to get an idea of what hell must be like. When we look at how lepers were tortured in body by the disease and then tortured in spirit and mind by the ignorance, rejection, and persecution from other human beings, we can understand why they were called the walking dead.

Leprosy as a disease is no longer the threat to humanity that it once was. Its causes and treatment leading to its arrest and preventing its further spread have been discovered. In time beliefs about its contagious character have been found to be untrue. But although leprosy as a disease is no longer a threat, leprosy as an attitude, leprosy as a social condition, is still a threat among us. There are still people we treat as lepers. There are still people we consider to be untouchable. There was a time when we considered the drug addict or alcoholic as untouchable. But drug addiction and alcoholism have touched so many of our families and have become so widespread, and we have seen so many living examples of people who have been delivered, praise God, that the drug addict and alcoholic are not the untouchables they once were.

For some, the homeless are the untouchables or the social lepers. We are embarrassed by them and offended by them. We don't want them around us, perhaps because they remind us of what we have been or could become and what some of us are perilously close to now. We can lose overnight what we have taken long to acquire. Some of us talk about "those people" or "the homeless" as if they are a different species. They are not. Talk to some of them and we will discover that in terms of background and dreams, some are very close to us and that but for the grace of God, there go we.

For a number of us, the new lepers or untouchables are HIV/AIDS patients. Human Immune Deficiency Virus (abbreviated HIV), which may lead to Acquired Immune Deficiency Syndrome (abbreviated AIDS) is a disease that attacks the body's defense systems, making them incapable of fighting infections. HIV is acquired in specific ways. It is acquired from unprotected sexual contacts or from the use of infected hypodermic needles. It is acquired from infected blood from transfusions. Now babies born to infected parents may have this disease.

Because this disease is so new to a number of us and because it is so devastating, like leprosy of old, much misunderstanding, misinformation, and miscommunication have circulated, causing hysteria and ignorant responses to it. Like leprosy of old, we stigmatize people with this disease. We talk about them in whispers. We pry into their backgrounds and personal business. We are afraid to touch them or come around them. We are ashamed to admit that either they have it or we have it. But the bottom line is that the person with HIV/AIDS is essentially no different from the rest of us in that they have a fatal disease and so do the rest of us. Ours is called living, because at some point we are all going to die of something. We are not hastening the day, but the fact is that the day is coming. It may come sooner for some than for others, but death is coming to all of us. God's Word reminds us that it is appointed that all people die, and after death the judgment (Hebrews 9:27). Before we judge somebody's character because that person has a certain disease, we would do well to remember that judgment belongs to God and not to us.

In the text, when the leper made the first bold move and approached Jesus, what was our Lord's response? Because he is the author and finisher of our faith, his response can serve as our example as we face the lepers of our experience. According to the text, Jesus had three responses. First, he was moved with pity. He was not moved with questions about how the person got it, but with pity. He was not moved with fear lest he get it. He believed too strongly in God's power to be afraid of any disease. He was not moved by popular prejudice or misunderstanding that told him that he could be defiled if he got too close. He was not moved with self-righteous judgment about the leper's getting what he deserved.

Jesus was moved with pity. Others saw a leper; he saw someone in need of love. Others saw vice; Jesus saw a victim. Others saw uncleanliness; Jesus saw someone in need of understanding. Others saw a hindrance; Jesus saw someone needing help. Others reacted in fear; Jesus reacted with faith. Others saw shame; Jesus saw suffering. Others saw a problem; Jesus saw possibilities. Others said "cast aside"; Jesus said "child of God." Others condemned, but Jesus had compassion.

Aren't you glad that pity is one of our Lord's attributes? When we recite Malachi 3:10 as we bring our tithes and offerings, the promise is that "I will open up the windows of heaven...". Heaven has a number of windows. Blessings come out of one window. Anointing comes out of another. Power comes out of a window. Glory comes out of another. Judgment comes out of a window and peace comes out of another and salvation comes out of yet another window. In the midst of all the other windows, I'm glad that there is a window called pity, grace, and mercy. I used to hear people say that God looked out of the mercy window one day and saw me where I was and picked me up and turned me around.

Jesus had pity on the leper. Then he made the second great move. He touched the leper. He touched the untouchable. I'm glad that I serve a Savior who is not afraid to touch the untouchable. When we read the Scriptures we note that this leper was not the only untouchable that Jesus touched. The woman with the issue of blood, the Samaritan woman at the well, the prostitute in Luke 7 who anointed him, Legion with his demons: all were social lepers that Jesus touched. Some would have considered Peter after his denial and Paul after his persecution as religious lepers that he touched.

Then some of us know that he touches untouchables not only because of what we have read in the Scriptures but by our own personal experiences. When we look at where the Lord had to bring some of us from, when we think about mistakes we have made, sins we have committed, weaknesses we have too easily succumbed to, promises we have broken—we could easily have been written off as untouchable. When justice and judgment said "untouchable," Jesus said, "They're not untouchable, just underdeveloped. So I will touch them with my redeeming power and cleansing blood so that they can become all they can be in me." Jesus said, "They are not untouchable, they are mine and I am theirs and I feel like the prophet Isaiah: 'Though their sins be as scarlet they shall be like snow' (Isaiah 1:18)."

When Jesus touched the leper he let him know that he still had worth and that he was still loved. If you know people with

AIDS, or who are substance abusers, or who have disgraced themselves, don't turn your back on them. God didn't turn his back on you. Don't leave them to suffer alone. God never left you. Reach out and touch them and let them know that they are still loved and that they still have worth. Sometimes they may pull back, but reach out anyhow. After all, God never stops reaching for us even when we pull back.

Jesus had pity on the leper. He touched him. And when he touched him in love, when he touched him in faith, a miracle happened—the leper was cleansed. Miracles can still happen when we touch in faith, touch in love, touch believing in the power of God, touch with determination that the devil will not have the victory. If Jesus could cleanse lepers in his day, I believe that in his name AIDS can be cured, cancer can be cured, arthritis can be banished, diabetes can be conquered, hearts can be made whole again, blind eyes can see. That's why we have to keep on touching and agreeing and not giving up on people because we never know through whose hands and whose faith God's power will work. Some will be healed and some will not. My business is to touch in faith and ask God for deliverance and let God determine who gets healed in this life and who gets delivered to the next.

Never underestimate the miracles that God's people can bring with a touch of faith. Sometimes people who are mentally off balance are described as being "touched in the head." We wonder why some saints act like they do. The answer is simple: They've been touched. We wonder why some people have so much wisdom and discernment: They've been touched in the head. We wonder why some people have so much love and so much joy: They've been touched in the heart. We wonder why some people have so much peace and so much patience: They've been touched in their spirit. We wonder why some people have so much fire and so much freedom: They've been touched in their soul. We wonder why some people can see things others can't see: They've been touched in their vision. We wonder why some people are so useful and productive: They've been touched in their hands. We wonder why some people are so determined and steadfast: They've been touched in their feet. We wonder why some people spread good news and encouragement wherever they go: They've been touched on their mouths.

How do I know God is real? I've been touched. How do I know Jesus redeems? I've been touched. How do I know the Holy Spirit fills? I've been touched.

Touched! Touched! Touched! Have you been touched?

Facing Success

Text: Matthew 21:10-11

How do we face success? How do we handle our blessings? Success and abundant blessings are greater threats to our religion and faith than hardships and doing without are. Most of us know how to live with trouble and hard times. A number of us were born in trouble, shaped by hard times, and raised on a steady diet of doing without. When difficulties arise we know what to do. We find our way to church; we become more prayerful; we start reading the Bible more often; we make all kinds of promises to God, to ourselves, and to others. We know how to say "Lord, have mercy." In times of trouble we know how to call on the Lord. If trouble lasted we would be paragons of virtue. But what happens to our piety, our promises, our prayer life, our participation, our righteousness and religion, when trouble lessens and the load lightens?

For many of us, piety is directly related to our problems and faith has a corollary with our fear. It seems that the only way the Lord can keep some of us humble and some of us prayerful is to keep us in trouble. Because God is gracious, however, "trouble don't last always." So the question for us is, "How do we keep our head on straight and stay focused and balanced when our blessings and our prayers are answered?" Or is our religion going to continue to be like a roller coaster, climbing up to its highest point when we're in trouble and falling down to its lowest practice when we think we have been delivered?

The day we celebrate as Palm Sunday was a moment of great joy for Jesus. In the Gospel of Matthew, the whole town is moved and Jesus immediately cleanses the temple. In Mark,

Jesus goes to temple and looks around and returns later to cleanse it. In Luke, Jesus weeps over the city of Jerusalem because its people did not know the things that made for peace and then cleanses the temple. In John, while Jesus' enemies declare that the whole world has gone after him, he goes on to predict his own death.

Although the writers of the Gospels differ in details about chronology and everything that happened on Palm Sunday, they all show that Jesus was not carried away with it. He was able to put praise in its proper place and keep his priorities in perspective. Praise is all right and everybody likes to receive it, but we have to live for something other than the praise of people. Praise of people is a great place to visit, but we can't make a home there. Praise is a nice snack, but it ought not be our main meal. Praise of people is recess in the school of life, but it is not the main curriculum. Praise is a good servant, but a terrible master. Praise of people is good medicine, but a terrible narcotic. It is a good prescription, but a terrible addiction. The trouble with a number of people is that they have allowed praise of people to become their main priority. When praise of people becomes our priority, we become their main priority. When praise of people becomes our priority, we become a slave to the group that we want the approval from. If people tell us to jump, we ask, "How high?" If they tell us to make a fool of ourselves, we ask, "When? Where? How long?" If they tell us to speak in tongues to prove we have the Holy Spirit, we ask, "When?" If they tell us to be petty or vulgar, we ask, "How low should we stoop?" If they tell us to pretend to be something we are not, we ask, "When should we go into our act?"

Praise from people is good, but like Jesus we have to put praise in its place and keep other priorities in perspective. After the Palm Sunday praise, Jesus went to the temple. He went from the streets where the voices of people were heard to the sanctuary where God was glorified. How do we handle praise and success? We keep God in perspective from whom all blessings flow. So when we receive a compliment, instead of letting it go to our heads we say, "Thank you, and to God be the glory." If someone says, "You look nice today," our response should be "Thank you, but to God be the glory, because this joy I have the world didn't give and the world can't take away." If someone says you sang well, spoke well, prepared a good meal, you did a good job, our response should be, "Thank you and to God be the glory, because God gave the talent and gift. I'm just trying to use what God gave me, and if it's been a blessing to you, praise God." If someone says you have a nice outfit or a fine car, our response should be, "Thank you and to God be the glory because if God hadn't blessed me, I wouldn't be able to buy what I have. I'm just another example and witness of how God will take care of you." Jesus could handle praise and success because he had another priority and that was the glory of God.

Jesus could enjoy great success because he had great standards. Some things he was not prepared to do. The devil promised Jesus the kingdoms of the world, if Jesus would bow down and worship him. Jesus told him, "Away with you, Satan! For it is written 'Worship the Lord your God and serve him only'" (Matthew 4:10). Like Jesus, we have to have some standards. If we don't take some stands we will fall for anything. Sometimes we have to say—even if it takes longer and the road is rougher, and we are misunderstood and mocked, and even if it means suffering and a cross—some things we are not going to do. We're going to worship and trust God, and if it doesn't happen God's way it just won't happen. But I don't believe that God will allow those who put their trust in God to fail.

Satan will seduce you even on good things if you allow him, and sometimes you just have to stand on your standards and say, "As badly as I want this degree, or as badly as I want this relationship to work, as badly as I want this promotion, as badly as I need the extra money, as badly as I want to be successful, I have great standards, and some things I'm not going to do."

Can't you see the three Hebrew boys standing before the great Babylonian king Nebuchadnezzar and saying, "We have no need to present a defense to you in this matter. If our God whom we serve is able to deliver us from the furnace of blazing fire and out of your hand, O king, let him deliver us. But if not, be it known to you, O king, that we will not serve your gods and we will not worship the golden statue that you have set up" (Daniel 3:16-18).

Jesus could face success because he was able to put praise in its place and keep his priorities in focus. He could enjoy great success because he had great standards. Then he could face success because he knew that fame was fleeting but that his heavenly Father was faithful. Success and fame have no loyalty.

They will lift you today and drop you tomorrow. They will love you today and leave you tomorrow. They will hug you today and deny you tomorrow. They will hallelujah you today and crucify you tomorrow. Think twice about giving up something or somebody who has a track record of faithfulness for somebody or something whose loyalty has yet to be proven or who has no loyalty. Many a person has dropped the loyal for the lovely, and the faithful for the fresh, only to come back to the faithful and loyal begging for another chance, because the lovely and the fresh walked out when the going got tough or when the thrill was gone. Be careful about forsaking a faithful God for a new promotion, new job, new degree, a new set of friends, a new love, new home, or new possessions. What you can buy for one price, somebody else can buy for a higher price. What is made in time will wear out in time. What you acquire by politics, sex, or promises, somebody else can acquire the same way. What you acquire by skill or merit, someone with greater skill or productivity can take away.

But I know a God who is faithful. Amidst the fluctuating circumstances of life, God is faithful. God's power is faithful: It wakes the sun up every morning. God's word is faithful: God keeps all God's promises. Jesus' blood is faithful: It still saves to the uttermost. The ministry of the Holy Spirit is faithful: She still empowers, enables and energizes, inspires and informs, guides and grants grace.

The Bible is the story of God's continuing faithfulness. Jeremiah declared, "The steadfast love of the Lord never ceases, his mercies never come to an end; they are new every morning; great is thy faithfulness" (Lamentations 3:22-23). The psalmist writes, "Yea, though I walk through the valley and shadow of death, I will fear no evil; for you are with me; your rod and your staff, they comfort me" (Psalm 23:4). Jesus said, "I am with you always, to the end of the age" (Matthew 28:20). Paul said, "I am persuaded that neither death nor life, nor angels, nor rulers, nor things to come, nor powers, nor height, nor depth, nor anything else in all creation, will be able to separate us from the love of God in Christ Jesus our Lord" (Romans 8:38-39).

How do we face success? How do we handle our blessings? Like Jesus, we do not let them go to our heads or turn them away from a God who is faithful and who teaches us what really matters in life. What really matters is not the television we watch, but the eyes that are watching us. Not what we buy, but the One who bought us. Not what we possess, but what possesses us. Not what we drive, but who drives us. Not where we live, but who lives within us. Not what we own, but who owns us. Not our dress, but our deliverance. Not our success, but our soul's salvation.

What really matters is the God who is faithful.

F — forgiving,
A — able,
I — independent,
T — true,
H — holy,
F — foundation and finisher,
U — understanding, and
L — loving.

God is faithful. Great is thy faithfulness.

Facing People Who
Do Not Take Us Seriously

Text: Luke 24:1-12

All of us at one time or another have had to relate to people who don't take us seriously. Have you ever been in the midst of a group of people or in a meeting and, when you make a suggestion or a statement, nobody pays you any attention? People keep on talking or debating the issue as if you have not said a word. Then all of a sudden someone else makes the same statement or suggestion, sometimes even using the same words, and people accept the idea or statement and act as if they had never heard it before: "That's a good suggestion! That's a great idea! Marvelous! Genius! What a novel or an original concept!" Meanwhile you can hardly believe what you are seeing and hearing because you're saying to yourself, "I just said the same thing ten minutes ago. Why wasn't it so marvelous and great when I said it?" You are amazed and frustrated that people would pay no attention to what you said, but all the attention in the world to what someone else said.

If you have ever had this experience of not being heard and believed, of not being taken seriously, then you can relate to how the women in the text must have felt. On the first resurrection morning Mary Magdalene, Joanna, Mary the mother of James, and other women who were at the tomb were asked, "Why do you look for the living among the dead? He is not here, but has risen. Remember how he told you, while he was still in Galilee, that the Son of Man must be handed over to sinners, and be crucified, and on the third day rise again" (Luke 24:5-7). The women told all of this to the eleven male disciples. And the Scriptures tell us, "But these words seemed to them an idle tale, and they did not believe them" (v. 11). The eleven male disciples did not believe the report of the resurrection because it came from women. In a male, chauvinistic world, women are still not taken seriously. It is still hard for some men to accept an idea if it comes from a woman.

Young people face the same dilemma. Society often believes that unless you have a certain amount of experience you do not know what you are talking about. Sometimes we forget that Jesus said, "Out of the mouths of infants and nursing babies you have prepared praise for yourself" (Matthew 21:16). We forget that at another time Jesus prayed, "I thank you, Father, Lord of heaven and earth, because you have hidden these things from the wise and the intelligent and have revealed them to infants; yes, Father, for such was your gracious will" (Matthew 11:25-26). We forget that Isaiah declared that "a child shall lead them" (Isaiah 11:6).

If you are a newcomer, people sometimes don't take you seriously. Revelation has to come from those whose favorite statement is "You just got here, I been here." If your educational or social background is not of the right degree or pedigree, then certain people will not take you seriously. They want to know by what authority do you do the things you do or believe what you believe. That was the question that people always asked of Jesus: "By what authority?" Instead of rejoicing in the power of God that Jesus displayed, they wanted to know by what authority he possessed it. Instead of heeding the truth he spoke, they wanted to know by what authority he spoke it. Instead of praising God for those whom he healed, they wanted to know by what authority he dared to heal.

With some people you have to have the right title or position or power for them to take you seriously. The story is told of an employee who refused to switch to a new insurance policy that was being offered by his company. Person after person came to him to try to persuade him to change, but his answer was always the same: "The old policy is fine with me and no one can force me to sign my name and change my policy." Finally, his boss came to him with an insurance form and a pen. He handed the policy and pen to the employee and said, "Look John, here's the deal, no signature, no job." The employee signed his name without hesitation. When some of his fellow employees laughingly asked him what the boss said that made him change his mind, John replied, "Nobody explained the policy to me like he did—no signature, no job."

People don't take others seriously because of misjudgment. First, they misjudge themselves, their sense of their own importance. Some people act as if they have a monopoly on truth and revelation. If the idea doesn't come from them, if they do not put their stamp of approval on something, then it's not legitimate or important or real. If it doesn't make sense to them, then it's not true.

Then, people misjudge you. They think they know the limits of your sense, your abilities, or your capabilities. People will tell you in a minute what you cannot do. Sometimes people's understanding of what you can or cannot do is based upon their perception of what they themselves cannot do or dare not try. You have to be careful about listening to people who tell you what you cannot do based upon their perception of themselves or you or God. Only you and God know what you, with God, can do. When you look at the size of the body of the bumblebee and the size and shape of its wings, you can only conclude that the bumblebee is not supposed to be able to fly. Flight for the bumblebee is aerodynamically impossible. But nobody told the bumblebee that it cannot fly, so it goes right ahead and keeps on flying.

A new minister, upon arriving at a church, was told that the bell in the tower could not be rung and could not be fixed. The tower was so old and the bell was so heavy that any attempt to fix it would either be too expensive or cause the bell to come crashing down into the tower and do irreparable damage to the church. So the bell remained silent in the tower for over thirty years because the foregone conclusion was that it couldn't be fixed. One day a new member joined the church and wondered what he could do about the silent bell. He did some investigating outside of the congregation and found that the bell could be stabilized with a very small investment of time and money. He didn't tell any of the old members about his findings, lest they tell him that the bell could not be fixed. So, because he didn't know that the bell couldn't be fixed, he went ahead and had the bell fixed. You can imagine the surprise on the old members' faces when they were sitting in worship one Sunday and heard the bell that could not be repaired, ringing to the glory of God.

Then, people don't take other people seriously sometimes because they misjudge God. We don't know who God will pour God's treasures into, God's dreams into, God's Spirit and power upon, and God's word into. For God does not see what we see. We look upon outward appearances, but God looks at the heart.

What do we do when people don't take us seriously? What did the women do when they were not taken seriously? They told their message anyway. They knew what they had seen and heard. They had been to the tomb, the disciples hadn't. They knew what the angel had told them, the disciples didn't. They didn't allow others who hadn't seen what they had seen or heard what they had heard shake their faith in what they knew to be true. If you have a dream or a vision, you keep your dream, even if others keep throwing up your past in your face, even if others don't believe you. If the Lord has changed your life, keep living your changed life, even if others don't believe, even if others keep expecting you to fall or fail or turn back to your former ways. If you have received the anointing of the Holy Spirit, keep praising God and exercising your gifts even if some people mock or falsely accuse you. If you have a testimony, keep telling your story even if some others don't believe it.

What do you do when others don't take you seriously? Dream anyhow, sing anyhow, serve anyhow, work anyhow, stand anyhow, survive anyhow, grow anyhow, achieve anyhow, graduate anyhow, build anyhow, love anyhow, work anyhow, succeed anyhow.

How have African Americans made it as a people? We have had an anyhow faith. People didn't take us seriously but we believed in our own possibilities anyhow. We believed that we were just as good if not better anyhow. We believed we were just as beautiful and just as talented anyhow. We prayed any-how because we believed that God took our pain and problems seriously and that he would hear and answer and make a way anyhow. People who believe in themselves don't refer to them-selves as persons with "attitude." When you believe in yourself, you don't have an attitude, you have altitude. You're looking up, not down. You're trying to elevate yourself, not stay where you are. When you have altitude you're not bitter, but better; not vulgar, but virtuous; not profane, but prayerful; not ignorant, but intelligent; not reckless, but wise; not demonic, but delivered; not defeated, but determined; not hollow, but holy; not a lowlife, but a lofty life; not mean, but merciful; not hell-bent, but heaven bound.

What do you do when people don't take you seriously? Take yourself seriously. What do you do when people don't believe in you? Believe in yourself. That's what the women in our text did. They told their story. The text says, "But Peter got up and ran to the tomb." I don't know why Peter went. Perhaps after his denial of Jesus, he needed a word of hope. If you take yourself seriously, somebody will hear you. Somebody will take you seriously. Maybe what you are saying or doing is the blessing or word of encouragement or hope that somebody's life needs at that moment. I know that we can be discouraged when folk are laughing at us and not believing our report. But keep doing what you're doing, somebody will get the message. Somebody will be touched. It may not be the one you expect. We may not reach the numbers we desire. But God will still use us to reach somebody who needs to hear our witness.

The women told their story and Peter was moved to go see for himself. But not only was Peter moved, later on Jesus himself showed up to verify what the women had been saying. I'm so glad that in life there is such a thing as later on. That's what the resurrection of Jesus demonstrates: that there is such a thing as a later on. The cross and crucifixion do not have the last word. Death and the devil do not have the last word. There is such a thing as a later on, when Jesus who was crucified shows up as a conqueror.

What do you do when people don't take you seriously? Take yourself seriously; keep doing what you're doing because somebody will hear you; and then wait for the later on—because it's coming! I don't know how long we'll wait, but it's coming. People may laugh at your dreams, but keep on dreaming because your later on, your justification, is coming. People may denigrate your sacrifices or your getting an education, but that's all right, your later on, your resurrection, is coming. People may mock your religion, but that's all right. Keep serving, keep working, keep glorifying God. Later on, Jesus is coming.

What is the last word that Jesus speaks in the Scripture? It is found in Revelation 22:20: "Surely I am coming soon."

Facing Yourself

Text: Matthew 26:69-75

James Baldwin, the noted African American writer, once said, "You cannot fix what you will not face." In this series of sermons we have been challenged and encouraged to face certain things in life and in ourselves so that we can either fix them or have them fixed. In this sermon we will be encouraged to face the most difficult person we will meet in life. The person who is our greatest joy and our greatest challenge, the person whom we know better than anyone else on the one hand, and yet a person who is a continuing enigma and mystery to us on the other. We need to face ourselves. If we are going to get the most from life itself, we need to take a good, hard, long look at ourselves.

This is a difficult task because it is easier to blame everybody else, including God, for everything that's wrong with us. Facing ourselves is difficult because sometimes we don't like everything we see when we face ourselves. But we have to face it to fix it. That was the reality that confronted Peter in our text. Earlier that evening at supper, Peter had expressed unswerving loyalty and undying commitment to Jesus. After hearing the shocking news from Jesus' lips that he would be betrayed by one of his own, Peter had declared: "Though all become deserters because of you, I will never desert you." To which Jesus replied, "Truly I tell you, this very night, before the cock crows, you will deny me three times." But Peter insisted, "Even though I must die with you, I will not deny you." The possibility of his denying Jesus was unthinkable to Peter. Yet in the text Peter denies his Lord and best friend, just as Jesus said he would.

Haven't we all been where Peter was? Haven't we all done

what was unthinkable for us and said we would never do? Haven't we taken things we said we would never take? Haven't we shown weakness where we believed our strength was uncompromised and shown compromise where we believed our steadfastness was persevering? Sometimes blaming others will not hide the defects that we are forced to face in ourselves. Peter, Jesus, and the Jews at that time were an oppressed people. The land of Palestine was under subjugation by the mighty Roman Empire. Roman power impacted the life of every Jew, even as white power and racism impacts the life of every African American today. But Caesar could not be blamed for Peter's denial that night. Roman power could not be blamed for Peter's disloyalty to his best friend. Peter had to carry the blame for his own weakness. Say what we will or may about the forces that war against us, each of us is responsible for our actions. At some point in life we become grown enough to make our own decisions and to be held accountable for our own actions.

We can't go through life blaming Mama and Daddy, our poverty, our background, our looks, our race or sex, or the system for everything that is wrong with us. At some point we decide whom we will serve and whom we will listen to. At some point we decide the kind of man or woman or boy or girl we will be. That's why before we can fix what is wrong in our lives, we need to face ourselves. Because often we are what is wrong.

The text says, "Then Peter remembered" (Matthew 26:75). Peter remembered how good the Lord had been to him and how patient the Master had been with him. Peter remembered how far the Lord had brought him since that day that Jesus had told him to drop his fishing nets. Peter remembered how the Lord had allowed him to see the daughter of Jairus raised, the Transfiguration on Mount Herman, and the agony in Gethsemane. Peter remembered the words of Jesus and was forced to look at himself. That's what the word of Jesus ought to do—force us to look at ourselves, not at our neighbors and their business, but at ourselves. Not at our enemies or the people we don't like and their faults, but at ourselves. Not at our family and friends, spouses or companions, but at ourselves. Not at the preacher or the other church members, but at ourselves.

When Peter looked at himself he didn't like what he saw. The Bible says that he broke down and wept bitterly. What do you do when you look at yourself and don't like what you see? One thing is for certain: You don't give up on yourself. That's what Judas did after he betrayed Jesus and realized what a dastardly deed he had done. He became disgusted with himself, his conscience revolted against him, his mind became so disoriented, his spirit became so sickened, his heart became so weighed down with guilt that he couldn't live with himself. He considered himself beyond redemption, forgiveness, and prayer, so he killed himself.

Don't give up on yourself. To do so is to believe that the hold of the devil is greater than the hand of the Deliverer, and that sin is stronger than salvation. Peter didn't like himself, but he didn't give up on himself. He went out and wept bitterly. He was turned inside out and outside in. I once heard a preacher say that Peter was converted that night and I believe him, because that's what conversion is all about—allowing conscience and the word of God to turn you inside out and outside in so that you can see for yourself what you lack.

When you take a good look at yourself under the conviction of the word of the Lord and see what you lack so that you can begin the process of conversion, the process of becoming a different person, then the word of the Lord can be a comfort. For on resurrection day an angel told the women, "Do not be alarmed; you are looking for Jesus of Nazareth, who was crucified. He has been raised; he is not here. Look, there is the place they laid him. But go, tell his disciples and Peter that he is going ahead of you to Galilee: there you will see him, just as he told you" (Mark 16:6-7).

Then, according to the Gospel of John, one day after the resurrection on the shore beside the Sea of Tiberius, Jesus asked Peter,

> "Simon son of John, do you love me more than these?" He said to him, "Yes, Lord; you know that I love you." Jesus said to him, "Feed my lambs." A second time he said to him "Simon son of John, do you love me?" He said to him, "Yes, Lord; you know that I love you." Jesus said to him, "Tend my sheep." He said to him the third time, "Simon son of John, do you love me?" Peter felt hurt because he said to him the third time, "Do you love me?" And he said to him, "Lord, you know everything; you know that I love you." Jesus said to him, "Feed my sheep." (John 21:15-17)

On the night that Peter denied his Lord, the word of Jesus rebuked him. But that morning, because Peter was willing to face himself, the word of Jesus rebuilt him, restored him, redeemed him, ransomed him, and reestablished him. The works of Jesus that had once shamed him now saved him. The word of Jesus that had once indicted him now inspired him. The word of Jesus that had once humbled him now hallowed him. The word of Jesus that had once lowered now lifted. The word that had once driven him to despair now brought deliverance. The word that had once brought tears now became his testimony. The word of the Lord that had once revealed cowardice in his character now produced a conqueror.

Well, the good news that I bring is that everything Jesus did for Peter, he is willing to do for you. If you are willing to face yourself, Jesus is able and willing to fix what's wrong. He's still in the fixing business.